Speak to Me

Also by Marcie Hershman

Tales of the Master Race
Safe in America

Speak to Me

Grief, Love and What Endures

Marcie Hershman

Beacon Press
Boston

Beacon Press
25 Beacon Street
Boston, Massachusetts 02108-2892
www.beacon.org

Beacon Press books
are published under the auspices of
the Unitarian Universalist Association of Congregations.

Printed in the United States of America

05 04 03 02 01 00   8 7 6 5 4 3 2 1

This book is printed on acid-free paper that meets the uncoated paper
ANSI/NISO specifications for permanence as revised in 1992.

Text design by Dean Bornstein
Composition by Wilsted & Taylor Publishing Services

Library of Congress Cataloging-in-Publication Data
Hershman, Marcie.
    Speak to me : grief, love and what endures / Marcie Hershman.
       p.   cm.
    ISBN 0-8070-2814-2
    1. Brothers and sisters.   2. Hershman, Robert—Health.
  I. Hershman, Robert.   II. Title.
  RC607.A26 H4674   2001
  362.1'969792'0092—dc21   00-012013

for Rebecca

Contents

Greetings

Not many people think of them these days, but most likely the two Voyager spacecraft are still up there, moving in silence among the spheres. Long ago both passed Jupiter, and the rings of Saturn. Then, dot by dot, the furious stammer of radio communication between craft and earth drifted away. If the calculations and trajectories held firm, each continued heading out-of-bounds: past snickerly, odd-duck Uranus and methane-soaked Neptune. Each also arced past Pluto with its pocked, black apple moons. Sailing out of our known solar system into whatever deeper space may be, but which we understand primarily as darkness, emptiness, and chaos, they are beyond any recall, save of our memory.

When Voyager 1 and 2 were launched into endless orbit in 1977, they carried the most sophisticated communication apparatus NASA could devise. The modules bristled with high-gain directional antennae, cosmic ray and plasma wave detectors, infrared spectrometers, television and radio electronics. What excited my imagination, however, was the small flat disk each also carried, an object recognizable to any teenager. A phonograph record.

Phonograph record! The term sounds as innocent and outmoded now as is the object itself. Yet back when vinyl platters hovered like flying saucers above the turntables of every home stereo, that twelve-inch, gold-plated copper disk was the gold record of gold records. It commanded respect. *The Sounds of Earth*, packed in a protective aluminum jacket, was meant to survive the abrasive glitter of space. The excitement for me in the Voyagers' venture was this: if, one long day, that disk got played. For impressed in its grooves was an audio story of human life — life on the one planet we know.

The Sounds of Earth holds in readiness music from Mozart and Beethoven; it holds Chuck Berry's rock-'n'-roller-coaster "Johnny B. Goode"; it holds the intricate gongs of a Javanese court gamelan and Australian horn and totem songs; it holds in suspension the songs of whales and summer winds, the percussive rhythms of horse and cart, horse and carriage, human footsteps, a grinding of automobile gears, echoes lifted wholebodied and translated as vital information via EEG and EKG.

And, intimately, the disk holds human voices. A thread of *hellos* called out in sixty different languages, starting with ancient Akkadian, spoken near the Tigris and Euphrates six thousand years ago, and ending with Wu, one of the many dialects of modern China. A roll call of welcome. A lilt of tongue and rumble of throat. Call it the sense and clear music of breath. Our human voices spinning out sound into the void. No, wait, not into the void. Only into a distance — one once as unutterable to us as the reality of any existence beyond our own.

According to NASA, it will be forty thousand years before the two Voyagers move within a single light-year of the star called AC + 79 3888. Then it will be millions of years before they near another planetary system. The projections assume that the small craft sailing through interstellar darkness have kept to their paths. Let's say they have done so. Let's say that although their sophisticated devices no longer sizzle, of the two, both still are out there. Moving in silence. Toward a great mystery.

Yet, it's those whose voices were impressed into copper and

gold whom I keep recalling. The individuals who one by one carefully enunciated into a microphone: *Bonjour! Salaam! Guttentag! Shalom! Hello!* What do they sound like now, these twenty and more years later? Where have their voices taken them? I mean, where here on earth? Or have they, as mortal voyagers, been given over to mystery, too? Their voices are still up there, out there. Ready.

The journey of a voice is the hope for connection.

Physical Realities

The spectrum of the human voice is like a fingerprint.
— DR. STEVEN ZEITELS

Speak to me.

Before you can say it aloud, before air stirs into sense above this page, you must think it. The impulse, desire as thought, flicks across the brain, and even the most scientific among us can't follow its routes. In the mass of gray sparking matter we all wear under our hats, the truth of transit remains hidden. Researchers have dissected the brain; computers have rotated and peered into the modeled sectors where thought appears as beads of light among the whorls; no one really knows what to make of it. There are some *ideas,* of course. The small patch of cortex controlling language is located — or usually located, we are told — on the dominant side of the brain; if you're left-handed that's the right side, right-handed and language streams from the left hemisphere. Broca's area, it's called, named for the French pathologist who discovered this bit of neural property and like any grateful, exhausted land-mass explorer, planted his flag, differentiating the place he'd seen and touched from that which he hadn't.

Further geographical coordinates inside and up top: in the folds of physical matter is an area (dominant side) that controls speech, and another that bursts into activity when the speaker tells stories (often, the opposite hemisphere). There is an area located midbrain, the transverse temporal gyrus, or bulge, that "listens." Somehow this slight protuberance translates the sensation of sound, the streams entering our ears, into mean-

5

ing. In other words, *ruff-ruff* comes clean: dog, barking, friendly — oh! welcome. In the middle of the brain are stored the identities of thousands of voices. The unique sweetness of voice, say, of someone you love. And the roughened words of someone you once loved. People you once loved. Voices of those individuals who might now be gone, disappeared in the flow of life through travels, time, death. Because of the brain's turn of matter inside, because of the secret activities it holds, you surely would recognize these voices still, if you could tag them out and hear them.

Speak to me.

The physical exercise of the voice involves a network of muscles, nerves, glands, impulse and agitation. Up from the lungs comes a blast of air. The air pushes against the vocal cords, which resist the pressure until suddenly forced apart. Opening and closing, the lip-like folds vibrate. Since sound is vibration, tone is the result. In what is usually the dominant side of the brain, especially in and about Broca's area, neurons fire, sending impulses to stretch the cords to heighten the tone, or perhaps to relax the vibrating cords and so lower it. In the resonant chambers of the throat, mouth, and nose, currents of air advance the sound, amplifying it. Put your fingers lightly to your own throat now, and you should feel this as you speak: a rapid oscillation, back and forth.

Consider that at the extreme of sixty vibrations a second a bass singer can maintain his lowest-pitched note, while the high C of a soprano will set the vocal cords swinging at least one thousand cycles a second. If just now you did not sing, but instead intoned: *aaahh!* in the familiar register of your daily speaking voice as if ordered by some doctor, then the rate might have been somewhere in the range of, say, three or four hundred vibrations a second. Each time we utter any bit of growl or nonsense, the waves feed back through our ears to our brain.

We match the sounds being made against the mental map of how we used to, how we always, how we *must* sound. Speak, and you play the present against the past. Utterance by utterance, you are tracking your own identity.

It all begins with desire, and with desire thought, and with thought and its mysteries the stirring of air. Voice is the assertion of presence. It makes the self's immediate claim: *Hear my voice. Hear me.*

The human voice rises from dual desires: to call other voices and lives toward it and to affirm the distinction of its own individual presence. Oddly, in evolutionary terms, voice grew out of a need to block, to cut off. We have no separate or discrete vocal organ, as such. The small horizontal cords set in the tract meant for the critical functions of eating and breathing originally were intended as safety valves. Between the mouth that chews and gulps food and the pink lobes of the lungs that draw in and expel air are the supple cords in their open-ended box, the larynx. The cords are to keep the passageway to the lungs free of debris.

The human voice is a by-product of physical necessity. And yet it is also an intricately personal construction. If on a physical level voice moves as sound — a stream of air and agitation — then it is in the realm of interpretation where it grabs hold. Voice stirs the emotions. It calls up time and our connections within it. It calls up life. No wonder we hope to hear certain people — spouse, sibling, parent, child, friend — speaking to us against long silence or across the breach of time.

Though the sound of an individual voice must prove as fleeting and mortal as the body that produces it, the spirit of a voice — the impress of personality it embodies — endures. Shall I say this simply? Loved voices echo.

Speak to me.

The personality of a voice arises from emptiness. The differences in the shape of a head and the differences in its resonant caverns and cavities — mouth, throat, and back of nose — make each voice unique. The cask shapes the wine, if you will. The bird, the fleeting song. We speak richly out of what is hollowed inside us. We speak as individuals, each distinguishable, because the personality of a voice, its lilt and color, comes from the spaces left open within.

Such emptiness is generative. Alive, it connects. Vibrant, both constrained and receptive, it shakes what comes into it, propelling it outward. Emptiness meant for creation. It is nascent space reverberating to the initial ping of an atom: *ahem!*, so that hence and henceforth and on and onward comes the swell and swirl of an expanding universe. This is the universe we call conversation.

We want to come into conversation, come into contact, come into voice. The desire begins when we are infants. No other animal has the babbling instinct, which is preparation for the complicated maneuvers of speech. Shaping sound into words takes work. It demands a concerted use of tongue, lips, teeth in order to produce more than a howl or a squawk. Adults lean over the crib rails and ask the infant, as if sensibly: *What are you telling me? You want me dress you? Then you want to go outdoors to go bye-bye?* Adults enjoy the ruse. And also want to believe: *Well, hey, how about that — talking with me!* Round and round, young and old, we converse. Words to babbling. Sense to nonsense. Voice to voice. Under this play is a serious wish: one day, we shall understand each other.

How nice that day is a long way off. How nice just to play, splashing about.

Until one day — and suddenly it is one day — one says: *Hear my voice. Speak to me.*

And the response comes back: *Here I am.*

Echoing Absence

The deeper the sorrow, the less tongue it hath.

— THE TALMUD

What first got me thinking about voice was its loss. A certain vibrancy, a particular tone, a word, a touch, love expressed through sounds — gone once, with a friend who moved, gone again with a brother who died, gone with the One whose face, if sometimes sensed through prayer, yet seemed turned, gone with a grandmother long receded and drowned in Alzheimer's fog. With each name I called out, absence replied. Absence was my question. And my answer.

I could think only that I ached to hear those I could not. I believed the connection to them was lost to me. The years following my brother's death got emptier and emptier. There is the emptiness that makes room for creation. Grief is emptiness of a different order. Grief empties inward. And constricts the throat, squeezes breath — makes it erratic. It scatters outward expression of thought as if scattering ashes. Grief is the cavern that closes down. Though it weeps, though it yells and gulps, though it recalls and beseeches, grief is voice stopped. Voice asserts presence; grief turns away. It embraces loss.

I'm sure if I were able to tell you about these years, if sitting face-to-face somehow we were able to speak beyond this page, you would say, *I know, I've heard that, too — the silence no one wishes to hear. I mean the voicelessness we fear will go on without end. That's what I mean.*

And your words coming toward me would ease the absence.

9

However briefly, sound would be solace. Speech would assuage physical grief.

Until recently, though, I would have neither sought nor imagined such a conversation because I no longer believed my place was here. Oh, I did not want to be dead, not exactly. But I also did not quite want to live. Even when I played the good sport, joining in with the jibes, laughter, ripostes, my voice was as hollow as my heart. That I would never again hear my brother calling to me. The hopelessness that nothing of us endured.

With that came shame. As my brother's body weakened, hadn't I seen his spirit grow wider? He was opening to his life as it was ending, while I who would live past him? I could not move. As if, if just one of us stayed still and remained closed, that might hold him.

There was so much I wasn't ready to understand. Much that I was both unwilling and unable to hear. How small the world is when we remake it solely as loss. And not a moment spent in it is quiet.

I missed talking to my brother. I missed the sound of his voice. I missed knowing the air would shake and the tympanic hammer in my ear *ping, ping, sing*. Against all rational sense, against the apparently physical limits of life on this planet, I longed for Rob's voice to surprise me. I wanted it to startle me awake as it had done so often back then, when time felt different and my life different, too — better, because my brother was in it.

I missed the sound of his mocking, sibling-smart laughter. "Why," he used to say, "do you have to dramatize every little thing, Sarah Bernhardt?" Dark eyebrows arched, he'd pause, shaking his head in amazed confirmation: yes, this was precisely how he'd expected I'd act. "Speak simply, be direct. People don't want to hear every detail. If you're telling a story, then tell it! Straight through, without flourishes. And don't get too personal."

Even when Robert was as old as he'd get — forty-one — he had a young voice. By this I don't mean immature or high-pitched, but alert to possibility, fluent with life. At the same time: steady and soothing. Here was a voice that imparted something more than its sound: the sense of its task. Of course when he spoke I leaned close.

I would ask him, only two years my junior, *What did you say, Robert?*

We had always been close. Ours was one of the lovely, subtle pairings that can happen in a family of six, with two active parents and four active kids. We were, the both of us, also our grandparents' children — close in a storied, Central European, almost old-fashioned way. Think of friendship as having the final edge over sibling competitiveness. Think how the relationship of brother and sister can be both a given and a gift; and how time can deepen the joy. *If he's too busy to speak now,* I'd say, phoning from my home in Boston to the television headquarters in New York City when he'd be working late on a film, *just tell him his sister called.* I rarely left my name; I left instead my relationship. He'd know. And not because, as the old joke goes, he had only one sister, but because in relation, it was he and I. He knew I would always be holding the other end of the line.

There are all kinds of families, and all kinds of bonds between siblings. It would take until we were both out of college in our mid-to-late twenties, when Robert and I each, separately, came out — to each other, and to parents, brothers, and the wider family. What a semi-shared sexuality (shared only in that each was different from the norm) contributed to the early bond between us, I can't say. I can pretend to know, but really I don't.

As a girl I had no idea, no overt feelings, of being lesbian. As for Robert, he later told me his experience was different: he did sense an attraction to boys and felt only friendly toward girls. However, ignorance of one's future self, and intimations of inchoate desires in one's present, do not a union make. What, then, did sexuality contribute to our initial closeness? The answers are: Well, something; and: Well, nothing. Maybe it just extended the same possibility for intimacy that heterosexual siblings have? An underlying empathy or compassion for the other's incompleteness.

In any case, I give voice to the idea of sexual orientation here because the times demand that I not stay quiet. Except in matters of white-glove etiquette, silence often will equal death. *Silence=Death* was the cry of the activist group ACT UP in the first decade of the AIDS epidemic, when the general public refused to speak about the virus out of a misguided hope that it was not infection but orientation that defined the disease. AIDS was the scourge that claimed my brother. With this as background, and foreground, here is what I can confirm with wholehearted honesty: Robert and I were close because we shared certain sensibilities. We loved those of our own gender. We loved learning. We gave ourselves up to the worded silences, in study, in prayer. We wanted to experience enough, and do enough. We wanted one day to have something of value to offer.

From the start and in our own ways, we both were eager to achieve. We dreamed about adding our voices to what seemed to us, in suburban Cleveland, the distant whirl of a dramatic world, gorgeous, sparkling lives. Unathletic, bookish, and in those horridly awkward, early-teenage years sullen, Robert was more private and self-protective than I. He sought refuge from the noise of our family — the usual mayhem of searching for lunch boxes and shouting the day's carpooling duties — through reading. No sports bios or kiddie-caper books for him; his imagination led him elsewhere. He stretched happily — with a child's grasp, of course — along the shelf of what was then confidently put forward as the classics. He began with the Greek myths and proceeded joyfully through Dickens, thence back to try to glean some sense from Shakespeare, a leap across the Channel when a bit more mature to visit Proust and Flaubert, and onward again to the great somber Russians. I was bookish, as well, but even to my own mind seemed less intellectual, for girls back then could be intelligent but not deeply ruminative, an essential qualitative difference. I chose to read American writers, for example. Dreiser, Steinbeck, Cather, Fitzgerald. That about says it. I was the home screen, though not Technicolor. (One long row we equally shared, trying to puzzle a way through the world: Aleichem, Malamud, Wiesel — Jewish writers, whose books seemed not to rest between borders.)

In general, I was more outgoing, quick to use humor as my right to stake a public place. I delighted in those bursts of laughter. How lightly they confirmed what I'd long suspected: witty girls might be heard, as well as seen. At those times, I'd sneak a glance at Robert, just to check. His response mattered. Oh, he'd *gotten* my turn of phrase, no doubt about that, but was he laughing? Had I made him laugh? Open unguardedly, throw back his head, and laugh? Or would he be holding himself very still, his face flushed with high color? Would he have that slight, sliding smile, contained and mysterious, which I recognized as a visual tone to his voice? A superior voice that seemed to be commenting as I turned to catch it: *Not again. You've said too much. Why do you keep taking center stage, Sarah B?*

I thought I knew how to read his voice in its myriad manifesta-
tions as I knew how to read the books I loved and the newspa-
pers delivered punctually, twice a day, upon our front doorstep.
Only recently did I learn from Robert's old college roommate
that I was mistaken about the smile I thought I saw when I'd
step forward. It wasn't that Robert considered me silly or shallow, but, as he confided to Tom in those sleepy conversations
that transform routine roommates into fast lifelong friends, in
measuring his voice against mine, he found mine the stronger.

"Rob worried about it," Tom said, blue eyes skimming my
face, reading it, too. "He thought his sister surpassed him."

Any jolt of pleasure I might have felt — Rob jealous of
me? — faded in the space of a breath. Stiffly I told Tom that he
was wrong, the equation was backward. It was my brother who
set the bar high.

"No, Robert said that you had your writing, but his work,
television . . ." Tom shifted uneasily. "Despite his successes,
what mark was he making? He was uneasy about it. He really
thought no contribution of his would last. He did worry, Marcie. Until the end. Then a couple of months before he died, he
called to say that whatever you and I wanted to do as executors
of his estate would be fine. If his journals or speeches could be
of use — if we could find a way to publish them or, say, place
them in some archives — good. If we could do nothing to preserve them, well then that was fine, too. The journals were
merely his way of keeping track of his life, but he told me he'd
finally moved on from that. He said he was able to put his faith
in what he had done in other ways, with his character. He didn't
need to keep track any longer." Tom paused. Awkwardly he
rubbed the back of his neck. "You don't believe what I'm telling you."

Although the responsibility of securing a public home for my brother's papers had just been lifted from me, I could barely look up. My dismay silenced me. I'd always been certain that Robert experienced our relationship as I did: we were different enough. And weren't competitors. And we took pride in — gained strength from — each other's dreams.

Aloud I said: "I don't understand. He knew that I counted on him. I admired him." The list streamed through my mind: Robert as high school salutatorian, Harvard polish and education, cosmopolitan friends, world travels. One of the gorgeous, sparkling lives. Producer of documentaries, winner of prestigious awards.

"Tom, I was the failure. I spent all those years trying for something and not getting anywhere. Three unpublished novels. Through it all, it was Rob who — well, Rob cheered me on." I said this last as a statement, yet the words wavered in the afternoon air as a plaint, as a: *Didn't he? You were at the sidelines. Didn't you see him?*

My brother's confidant, my new messenger, tightened his lips. He nodded, just once. "He did encourage you. He wanted you to be happy."

Useless dismay, to find out we had squandered our time together. Rob, upset about the strength of his voice against mine? What could he have been thinking?

And, more, why didn't he just say something? We could have had more. We would have talked. We would have set things to rights.

Roughly I demanded just that. Why. Why didn't Robert speak to me?

Leaning back in the green overstuffed chair, Tom sighed. The summer sun flooding through the front window striped his shirt, falling across his chest as a single sash. "He didn't, because he couldn't." He held his breath an extra beat. "He wasn't proud of being envious. Besides, it wasn't all he felt for you. He also hoped you'd find success."

The bond between siblings is corded by numerous strands. We are born into our relationship with one another. As innocents we toddle toward the most intimate history. Daily, little by little, we make nice, we pummel, we hold hands crossing the street, we separate and run, run, run away faster. *Can't catch me.* That early, caught up in the present, we create a future. Throughout the years to come, these are the moments we'll mean when we say: *family.* The full moments we'll feel when speaking aloud the words: *my sister, my brother.* That early on — yes, we become vocal as siblings. We wake to a circle of whispers, laughter, fights, shouts. We absorb the same secrets and stories. Later as adults if we wish to come close again to that past, we turn to one another for confirmation and ask: Remember? Oh, surely you remember. Or we ask to hear a tangled tale we sensed, for good reason or ill, we hadn't been told, not then, not that early on. Siblings are our witnesses in time. To our times. So we can turn and ask, too, about a golden-lit day that still shines whenever we glance back for a look. We keep wondering, tell us, if in fact it really happened.

Family. Sibling. Brother. Sister. Home. Combustion, propulsion, gravity, and time set us in each other's path, and for at least a while we orbit in common a fiery sun. In an ideal paradigm we would travel most of the fleeting journey together — if not side by side, then every now and again passing closely enough to be within reach. For all that and more, the breaking away — the absence through death — of a sibling is painful in ways for which we can neither prepare nor expect. Still, there it is. Silence as real as a lit day.

* * *

I missed the sound of Rob's whispering, arguing, outbursts of joy, singing. And the still side of conversation, I missed his listening. Sure, listening is part of a voice, as well. Consider its sound as an exhalation not fully let free, a non-interruptive *hmhh* clipped at the end a half-step or a half-note up. The tilt and increased force indicating surprise. No fooling? Or praise. How wonderful! Or skepticism. Are you certain? A slower half-tonal step down in exhalation, and the conversation played back to the speaker is nearly said to be somber. The sound of a listening voice is subtle. Once you've heard it, heard how its qualities vary from person to person, then you know the first secret of eloquence. What I am trying to say is simply this: the human voice is never more beautiful than when it has stretched its breath, both ways.

Isn't that why when things get rough or impossibly, giddily wonderful, you search out X to tell all about it? You can't wait to call up X, want to run over and see X. It is X, whose voice is full and heart and mind are open — X, the one to whom you want to spill out your dreams.

My brother was X.

For so long, for all our once-lives.

Listen: Not suddenly but as we were dreading after the years of balancing stalwartly, precariously, with grace or great difficulty, between health and illness, he was gone. The earth fell over him then; air spilled without him. The voice I'd heard soon after forming my first words, the voice I'd leaned against, the voice I meant I wanted when calling out loud for my brother, did not stir.

And there is this, too: I missed the sound of my own voice, in relation to his. Here was his voice, too. Hear it as the voice of relation — for in mine had been ours. I mourned my full voice, silenced by halves.

What springs to mind is something about loss Robert once told me. Maybe we had this conversation while he still lived in New York, the ultimate city of realism if one is ill, with its over-crowded hospitals, and difficult to hail-and-halt transporta-tion, and its four seasons — one of which is long winter. Possi-bly our discussion took place after he moved to California. I don't know; I'm not sure. Certainly it was well before, a long year or two before, he died too far away on the other side of the country. In any case, we likely were talking over the phone, because I can't see his face or any his gestures. I don't see us in physical relation to one another during this particular exchange.

Still, let's say: a phone call. Let's say Robert was speaking to me through the thinnest of wires from a place so distant it might as well have been immaterial. I do recall his voice was braced by an urgent force, as he said: "Listen, Marcie!"

Then everything stopped for a moment. Hacking, one growling cough and gasp after another, to clear his throat of the phlegm. "Wait," he managed. "Will you wait — ?"

I always tried to sound nonchalant while hearing him strug-gle. "Um-hmm." Coil by coil, I played the cord about my fin-gers. "Hmm?" The wet web flung up from his lungs kept trap-ping words and breath.

In a burst of static, Rob's voice shook clear.

He told me how angry he had been at himself. He'd wake each day berating himself for what he used to be able to do: used to be able to wake in the middle of Manhattan and run five miles, used to be able to work flat-out to produce difficult tele-vision documentaries — research the topic, find those people who had stories to tell or to hide, write the questions for CBS's telegenic interviewers to ask animatedly on camera; used to film; used to work in the editing room well into the evening;

used to watch the finished story air on the network screen; used to travel; used to meet up with friend after friend, talk whole nights away, eat with pleasure; used to sleep, dream, and wake rested. Rob said he had gotten so angry at not being able to do any of this anymore that he did nothing else but rage against the losses. "But — " he said, then had to halt.

I stopped breathing, lips pursed above the black mouthpiece.

A moment — two — passed. Clear again, Robert said carefully, "But you have to start from where you are." He meant that he wasn't going to berate himself any longer for having lived a life he had enjoyed, a life where he achieved the things he'd always wanted. He was going to acknowledge the present, then sit up. He was going to move in a new way — small gestures — right here.

I can almost hear him again in the effort to keep a passageway open, then hear the release of his breath, signaling and unlocking my own. But I can't quite hear his voice; I can only remember it, a memory made not from sound but from narration and description, the timbre and rhythms culled from a short list of traits. The vibrations of Rob's voice sounded: youthful. Beautifully balanced. Clean at the center.

My brother was speaking through wires, from some spot hundreds or thousands of miles distant. He was telling me how he could live. He was telling me what it takes over time, with each mouthful of breath, for any person to start.

And again, start.

I want you to know: the mistake I made during the years of my grieving was in believing that my memory is where his voice ends. That memory following long illness must mimic illness. That absence echoes all.

In the Dark

From the depths, I have called to you. . . .
— PSALM 130

The invitation is to recall darkness. The intention is not to frighten, but to reintroduce and thus renew our relationship with the balm of deep shade in which we spend, by means of constancy and repetition, a good half of our lives. Not the better half of our lives, mind you, but an essential half. Darkness has the power to disturb us, and when it disturbs it makes a demand: *Speak — and unsettle me.*

"I would call out for my father if I awoke in the middle of the night," said my friend Judy. "Afraid, maybe of a shadow crossing the ceiling, I'd just scream for him. I wouldn't stop to think about what I was doing. I'd sit bolt upright. 'Dad,' I'd yell. 'Daddy!' Then out of the dark would come the three most comforting words I've ever known. 'Here I am,' he would call. Sometimes, that was all I needed to feel safe. I just wanted his voice, wanted his response. After that, I could shut my eyes. How I long to hear him saying those words once again," she said.

Gently she replaced the white porcelain cup into the center of its saucer. The restaurant we sat in was filled with brightness and chatter. Judy looked over my shoulder. She blinked rapidly, as if surprised by an image she did not want to see. I knew that her father, ailing for years, now lay in a coma. At the near-end of his life, the shadows that frightened her had moved somewhere deeply within and at no time of the day or night could he be roused. She visited as often as distance and schedule allowed. She sat at his bedside. Hoping that he might be able to hear and understand, she called to him quietly. She turned her face toward the darkness alive between them, saying, in effect, he didn't need to cry out, and: now she was here.

Her voice was her gift. It was also his echo. The sound of her words, breath in breath, led her toward him — through the narrowing corridor, unlit, where he lay and where she was yet scared to go. She said that as she spoke she believed somehow he heard her, and so she kept on. There was the rustle from some other room, one not far away, of another voice, calling.

Our voices are lights. They illuminate the darkness with beams of sound. They fly into the unknown, bodiless, unguarded. They are verb rather than noun, movement rather than object. In the dark they are who we are when we move past our names, up from the nameless place inside, heart beating, and onward, outward, into what seems a void.

Think of a starless night. Think of diving into the black pool. Think of the water sliding over your head, face, neck, fingers, palms, arms, stomach, genitals, thighs, knees, toes. Think of yourself as immersed, breath inward, body thrumming; and think of how you break the surface in one bright burst. You see (even without a moon) the world is new, and yet returned. That is how our voices move in the night. Swimmer, swimming us. Swimmer, carrying us through an immersion in which we believe we cannot draw another breath, and yet survive.

> *The plagues of darkness:*
> *Darkness of fear.*
> *Darkness of failure.*
> *Darkness of pain.*
> *Darkness of uncertainty.*

Darkness of betrayal.
Darkness of loss.
Darkness of vision as emptied faith.
Through all this flies our voice.

Out of darkness and void, so we have been told, came light and then entire worlds. Out of thickest night, which was Nothing, *ex nihilo,* came a first command. Spoken into the void: "Let there be . . ." Let there be this, and this, and this; and, ah yes, also this. Call it the sound in all-emptiness of some permission, granted. Call it the impulse, impossible to forbid, startling creation. Or if you are so inclined, call it *ping,* that first spring into matter and substance of energy, a restlessness toward greater shape of that which is so infinitesimally minute as to seem barely an itch between not-visible and invisible, and yet which, we are told, exists. The scientific among us classify such fleet sparks as particles: subatomic; they further dub them: quarks, whirlimagigs, zippy mini rocky-roller-coasters, teeny-tiny-teensy-clanging-chimes, and not-ever-gonna-be-electrons swingin' on a string theory. Or, they ignore what is small to land right in the center of the bloom, in the first widening moment after no-moments, and call that: Big Bang. I call all of it: the introduction into the universe of conversation. You may state your own preference based on belief or rationale. The first word is: *Let.* And implicit in the word is an initiating voice, inviting response.

The page between us is swept with light. It's likely that you're considering my invitation to dissect darkness while sitting in an armchair or lying along the curve of a couch, the rounding glow of a lamp close by. Could be (and this is a universe, anything is possible) you're balancing upright while traveling by bus, and the words on the page won't keep still;

they shiver. You try to keep your footing secure; you have one hand gripping the book's spine, the other stretched above your head, clamped to a swaying strap as the cumbersome vehicle lurches in response to a city's synchronized glitter. Or, you are wedged, shoulder to jowl, on a subway car hurtling through the dry dark throat of a tunnel. Tunnel after tunnel takes you, reading. For a moment, you lift your head in response to your own half-cry inside; you almost remember something you once heard, or perhaps you did not hear it, but only saw the words written; for a moment you remember the phrase: a web, flung up from the lungs. Then you are swallowed, you inside the flickering tube, and there is nothing outside but black, and shuss, whish, clackety-clack. You travel farther along in silence, holding words up to your face. You are reading this book beneath the surface of a world itself spinning, half lit, half diminished, through space.

If there is anything in the universe that does not travel at least part of its route through darkness, I don't know what it is. Illuminated by degrees; shrouded by degrees.

Risk it. Now, at my urging: for a moment, shut your eyes.

Why won't you now at this moment shut your eyes?

You. With the book in your hand. What is it you think likely to happen if you stop reading these words? We will be cut off. A darkness fallen between us.

From inside you?

Inside, will there be only darkness? Or might there be, too, a world lit by degrees? And a voice there, already flying? Already *ping*?

Let me suggest that if at the end of this sentence you do shut your eyes, the voice you will hear without hearing, as your eyes, closed, see without seeing, well, it will be one of those you've been listening for since you first cracked open our book; now, go dark.

"Halt!" shouts the sentry. "Who goes there? Who breaks the silence this black night? Who is it? Tell me the password."

Speak. Say who you are. This is the first demand of the guard defending a territory believed ringed by invaders. It is the cry of those granted sight only by sound.

I remember the night my brother ran away. He only ran away once. He wanted to leave all of us because he was a child. Barely ten years old, he didn't stop to think how separation felt. He didn't think about anything but the angry sting of one moment. That evening when our father berated him, Robby shouted back. Pushing up out of his chair, he turned and walked out of the house. Which door he left by, I no longer recall. There were five doors on the first floor, not counting the one in the west wall of the garage. Three solid wood with brass hinges, and two double plate glass and sliding; all led at varying angles to somewhere outside.

Let me back up.

I come from a family of talkers. Not chatty people — no, but storytellers and argument makers. People with confident viewpoints. I grew up amid the sound of words jostling for space in the air, words as vigorous and vital as the people who formed them. Those were the years when Dad's voice roared without challenge. Tease a sibling, rise too slowly to clear the dinner glasses and dishes, forgo common courtesies, or simply act in the wrong, and his voice, primed for fight-and-not-flight, shot into sound. *What's the matter with you? Don't you know what's right?* Or: *Stop that. Enough!* Mom's voice was as she was, quieter. She'd have her hands immersed in a sink of warm water, and her words seemed liquid, too, clouded and swirling. We could hear her calling above the shussing spray from the kitchen faucet: *Come back here to help me, someone. Come back and help. Marcie, Robby?* (Only rarely did she call to Cliffy or Danny — at six years and three, too rambunctious to wield a small towel in careful circles over the slick surfaces of wet china plates.) *Not me, Mommy. It's Robby's turn,* I might say. Robert would counter: *Nope. Marcie's. I helped last night.*

When our grandparents came by to share a meal, which was nearly every Sunday and on Fridays for Sabbath dinner, Nonny dispatched with the chores before anybody, including Dad, thought to lean back from the table and point out what needed doing. For Nonny, completion in the kitchen was a matter of pride. *All done but the shouting,* she would declare with brisk satisfaction. She'd glance brightly over the bare counter, and replace the damp towel, folded in quarters, over the edge of the white porcelain sink. *Now, who wants to take a nice stroll around the block with me?* She'd nod first to Papa, whose quiet smile bespoke his gentleness, then she'd sweep her eyes around to the rest of us. *Who wants to walk and talk and hear stories? You know what I was thinking about today? How Papa and I almost went to live somewhere else, not Cleveland. We wanted to start our new life, but where to go? You don't know where? Far away. Come, and I'll tell you.*

Most of the time it was just Dad, Mom, Robby, Cliffy, Danny, and me in the house. Of course laughter was a daily companion, as well. So, too, the solitude accorded by study; that necessary quietude settled in with me whenever I sat back with a book in my favorite chair. Set at a remove from the main action, the chair stood in the den angled before the pair of sliding glass doors. Our backyard — flat, green, and tended — stretched beyond, ending at the very un-suburban vertical uproar of what we called "the woods." It was in the woods where my brother tried to disappear.

The cause of his leave-taking was as common as it was

abrupt. Like most arguments, this one started at dinner. We were around the kitchen table, the six of us. Dad sat at the head, the windows streaked blue with twilight at his back, and at the foot, with the hallway entry open behind him, sat Robby. You would think the foot was where Mom would have been, given the tradition of husband and wife anchoring the table and, by extension, the family, but she was one position off. She sat along the right side, next to me; Cliffy and baby Danny sat on the side opposite, their chair backs not far from the inner wall.

Dad had just picked up the server from the bowl of potato salad. The big serving spoon was coated with eggy-yellow mayo. As he dug into the chunky mound, he asked over our chatter, "Who else would like to have seconds?"

I heard Robby say, "Me, Daddy. I'll take it."

The spoon handle clinked against the rim of the bowl. Dad said coldly, "Don't talk with food in your mouth."

There was a slight pause in the action. You could feel it, a stillness sliding about the table. One by one, like zebras at the watering hole, we lifted our heads at the shift of scent in the air. He might be there in the tall grasses by the fallen tree. Best to stay quiet, pretend nonchalance. He could lose interest, or mean nothing by inching closer. A big warm cat, padded-pawed, he could just as often be playful. I glanced sidelong at Robby; he was still chewing. Staring straight ahead, his thin face flushed. His scalp shone pale amid the short brown bristles of hair. Butch cut, it was called, but because you could see his scalp and any imperfections and bumps in the shape of his skull, the effect of the style on him was anything but butch. Assertive vulnerability, maybe.

Awkwardly I reached across for the potato salad. The chilled aluminum bowl was heavy, requiring both hands to pull nearer. "May I have the spoon, please," I said, sitting up straighter, "to pass it to Robby?"

27

Dad said quietly, "That's disgusting." His chin jutted, pointing. He didn't gesture with the spoon in his hand, which would be poor manners. "You're chewing with your mouth open. What's wrong with you?"

"Nothing's wrong with me," Robby muttered, ducking his head toward his plate.

"Oh yes, something is."

Cliffy giggled. So did Danny, who began to rap his fork against the table's edge.

"I can see everything getting mashed in your mouth. It's disgusting."

"Gene — " Mom said, and for a moment he glanced her way.

"What?" he demanded. "What? You don't sit where I do. You don't have to look at him every night."

Shaking, Robby pushed back his chair.

"What are you doing?"

"I don't want you to have to watch me, eating. I'm not going to stay here."

"Good," Dad said flatly.

"And, you know, I don't like how you talk to me." Robby tugged at his T-shirt, pulling at the looseness of the cotton, as if he needed it to fit more closely against his body. His chest was heaving. "I'm getting out of here." His voice sounded as if he were tugging it closer, too; quieter at the end of the sentence than at its start.

Dismissively Dad waved and a chunk of celery and mayonnaise fell from the serving spoon onto the tabletop. "Go."

"I am," Robby said. "I'm leaving." Then, whether he purposely let his jaw drop or whether he was as surprised by what he was about to do as the rest of us, his mouth opened. It was wonderful and horrible to see behind his teeth: a mess of liquid and solids, and half-buried tongue, and gleaming flesh. In the next second, grimacing, he clamped his jaws shut and stalked from the kitchen into the hall.

We sat in silence with only the staccato beating of the baby's fork tines against wood. Six raps, two, a flurry of five.

Dad turned to his left and said through tight lips, "Stop it. You've wrecked the table." His face was drained. "Stop that, Danny, or I'm taking the fork from you."

"You'll have to eat with your hands," Cliffy teased, poking his brother with an elbow.

"No," cried Danny. "No, no, no, no, no."

"Quiet," Dad groaned, leaning forward.

I didn't hear Rob's footsteps, nor the clicking of any door.

Mom left the table. She went to the entry. As if she weren't looking for him, as if this were all she'd wanted to do, she leaned against the wall and raised her hand to the switch. Yellow light fell like a cloth over the table. "Oh!" one of the boys said under his breath. The five of us stared at each other, blinking. It had gotten dark inside so quietly, we hadn't noticed. Mom still had her palm raised against the small panel.

Dad looked down and shook his head. He stuck the server back in the aluminum bowl. "It's all right," he said, after a moment. "Let's finish dinner."

"Who wants more of the chicken?" asked Mom, coming back to the foot of the table. Gently she leaned over Rob's chair, her shadow covering his place. She looked about our diminished circle, hopefully. "Both wings are still here."

No one spoke up.

"Send the platter around, Phyllis. Someone will take something." He turned. "Marcie? Cliff, Danny, what do you say? A little more?"

There was a rush of wind through the high trees. I glanced past Dad. The glass panes behind his chair reflected: his shirt, the flickering shine of reaching hands and bobbing heads, the lamp's halo, the sheeted glare of one interior wall. Those were the only pieces of our family visible. I looked through them and into the night as far as I could.

"Robby!" I yelled, standing up on my pedals. The bike coasted over a crack in the sidewalk. "Rob!" I was embarrassed to shout when the streets were obviously empty and my cry could carry into the houses, but he'd been gone too long for a prank. I'd ridden the mile-long loop of blocks a few times already. Everyone heard. Everyone knew: Robby was gone. Robby didn't reply. He didn't shout back. They knew because the girl's voice streamed close and faded; twenty minutes later, streamed close and faded, and with each round she sounded less sure and more shrill.

The darkness that had been porous and sweet and warm when I'd started out was different now. When I first began looking, I headed immediately for my best friend's house, full of jokey self-importance as I reported how my brother had run off, and though he was probably on his way back, would they please keep an eye out for him? But those minutes on their doorstep happened hours ago, when the air still held the last of the twilight, a streak of pearl. Now I stood pumping the pedals, arms out straight, gripping the handles, front spokes blurring like ink, and the dark seemed airless and opaque as the same silhouetted trees, hedges, set-back houses came around again.

"Robert!"

Let me stop.

Let me stop and go inside where the bed is wide and familiar, the walls high, and the windows cracked just enough for the outer world to whisper some secrets. I have washed up and climbed in. I have shut my eyes at the urging of our parents, who are themselves tired and who inadvertently showed me how frightened they are, too, by their unsteady smiles. The boys — that is, Cliffy and Danny — have been in their beds in their room for a long time. Could be they even are sleeping. The lights are off on the second story, the sleeping, private level.

Below, a big silver-gray car is parked in the driveway. Nonny and Papa drove over at some point earlier while I was uselessly cycling the streets. I can hear my grandmother now. She's saying that Robby is a good boy and he will come home, she is sure, as sure as she is of anything in life. I can hear my mother asking the time, then with a small moan: *11:38?* My father's voice: garbled and slow as if moving underwater and caught inside bubbles, a burst of anger, a word: *idiot;* a phrase, *I didn't mean;* later: *wrong, sorry;* then: *idiot,* again. Odd pairings. Mom: *Gene, oh — they're here.* Footsteps, hurriedly through the front hall. The door opens as my father goes out to meet the police officers just pulling in. The red lights race across the walls, then go dark in a kind of code. No longer the center of my own attention, I am upstairs, in my room off to the right side of the hall, being very quiet. I try to keep track: one, in the driveway, two, downstairs, two in bed. And somewhere out in the verticality, out in the darkness, out in the silence, too distant for us to hear him, our grandfather in his white shirt, pressed gray slacks, and dress black shoes is batting his way through the woods.

This is the wrong place for him to be, just as it is the wrong terrain for his grandson. If he looked back behind him, the house's lit windows would be fractionally visible, but he heads in deeper. He passes the pear tree with its deceptively thin, crooked black limbs. He steps into the cold mud of the woods' rubbishy stretches. What made him think the wildness is refuge for a bookish boy, when the police are searching shopping areas and the transit lines into the city? Or is it his rationale

31

that a person in trouble seeks immersion in that which is for-eign? The underbrush rustles in an unpleasant flood; heavy-bodied rats — he has seen isolated brown rodents streaking confusedly across the family's back lawn in daylight, now he hears a raft of them racing away as he enters their territory.

Dry-mouthed, he stumbles across a ditch, bruising his out-stretched palm on the rough bark of a pin oak. He looks up through branches to find drifting, glowering clouds. The star-less heave of the sky dizzies him. He is sweating down the back of his neck and under his shirt, despite a cool breeze. Bending, he extricates his left pants leg from its sticking points along a vine studded with prickers. Does he hear something as he straightens? Moans, inarticulate but human? How frightened his grandson must be. The boy must have a will of iron to hide himself in such a wood at night. He must have a pride and anger that no one suspected. Yes, he has been hiding himself for a long time, it seems, right in the midst of the forest of fam-ily, if he could run off, and keep to it, this long in the dark. A length of darkness that, he himself knows from experience, is not even that long at all.

He tries to focus his eyes to distinguish between tree limb and shadow, but, no. Stung, he takes one more step to be free of the ropy tangle of teeth. "Robby, where are you?" he shouts, hands cupped, directing his words as if through a megaphone. "Where are you? This is Papa! Come back. You're breaking our hearts." Holding his breath, standing in place — out-of-place — in the woods, he tilts his head, straining to take in some re-ply he can understand.

I am quiet and not asleep, straining to hear his voice from this distance. It is so many years later, and both he and Robert are gone. My voice, calling out in the night, is my gift. It is also his echo: the awed *o* of grief in *Robby*. The dread-pounded and repeated *a* in *Papa!* Hiccups of fear in *Come back*. And as for *breaking our hearts* — the whole phrase said quickly is syncopated like a pulse. My grandfather's faithful pulse. He parted the awful dark in our family's first search for one whom we believed, prematurely, we had lost.

Sometimes, if I put down the book, if I shut my eyes to pay attention, my grandfather's voice flies through the wood to find me.

He moves on. He will keep calling out these same phrases, though he can't see where he is going and though he fears that no one will hear him. He wants to find his grandson who might be in here, in this strange dark place, too. He can't be sure.

By the middle of the night startled cries erupt in the next room. I don't look at the clock to see the exact second this happens. I know only that my eyes have snapped open and fastened on the golden line beneath the door. I get up, feeling my way. The hallway is burning with light. I need only round the corner to confirm by sight what I've already been listening to: my brother's sobbing, my parents and grandparents surrounding him, weeping. I stand in the doorway and can see them holding each other. In such a small space the light arches, vaulting over them all as if this child's bedroom is domed and the babbling within it of their relief and forgiveness, their welcome and sorrow, is a prayer sent out to the darkness and, in the same moment so unspeakably fleeting and bright, also held close.

Repeat after Me

My friends — .

— FRANKLIN D. ROOSEVELT,

addressing listeners of his radio-broadcast "fireside
chats" during the Depression and World War II; heard
again via tapes preserved in the National Archives

(REEL SIX, SIDE A)

When my brothers and I were growing up, Euclid Beach
Amusement Park still stood on Cleveland's shore of Lake Erie.
Even back then, the park seemed a relic from another, more
wonderful time. That immense sprawl and scale, the great
landlocked piers of wooden girders rising into hills of rattling
tracks, calliope music wheezing from the center drum of the ca-
rousels, we knew little to rival it. The air smelled of lake water,
popcorn, and spun cotton candy — old-timey smells. Though
we never saw them, men in straw boaters and striped shirts
were strolling by, ladies in wide-brimmed hats and long
dresses fanned themselves in the shade of the elms.

Among the crowd of kids in cotton T-shirts, Bermuda
shorts, and U.S. "jump higher" Keds, Robby, Cliffy, Danny, and
I tugged on the hands of our be-sandaled mother and white-
buck-shoed father. How slowly they talked! They spoke about
watching out for each other, about not going on rides alone,
about holding hands when people tried to push past in a crowd.
Oh, they were repeating themselves. We begged to run off. We
wanted to run and ride and scream until, overexcited, we exhausted ourselves.

We raced into line at all the best sites. The high hill thunder of the Thriller roller coaster and the plunging, thirsty splash of Over the Falls. The neck-snapping jolt of the Dodge-'Em rubber bumper cars and the *whoosh* out over the lake of the cable-strung Rocket Ships. Everyone shrieked, we were traveling faster and faster, sliding the chutes of the Flying Turns or crashing through black swinging doors inside the Laugh in the Dark. Some attractions were frightening. Some were silly. All made us laugh. We laughed because, as we clambered inside linked cars to chug slowly up the incline of that first steep grade, we couldn't forget about the descent. Each ride had it, the instant when the floor dropped away, when the sky opened, when the wind roared from everyone's mouth. The thrill came in the second between knowing — and going. Carried toward that one moment we could never predict, we leaned forward, expectant: oh, zigzag of joy.

Excuse me, I meant to get right to the point. I meant to let go of their hands and deposit these four dusty children back on their own at the feet of Laughing Sal. This is where they always want to go after the rides, and where through the concession stands and hurly-burly they always ask to be led.

Now then: Marcie, Robby, Cliffy, Danny stand absolutely still, facing the left-side arch of the arcade as Laughing Sal, jerking and swaying behind the glass pane, towers above them. In her blowsy Depression-era housedress, and thick black practical shoes, Sal rises over six feet tall. She is broad waisted and buxom, her hair wild red, her skin pale as death, her gap-toothed smile garish as any clown's. But she's not a clown, can't be, for out of her mouth ripples the most mellifluous and richly chorded, most gorgeously glorious womanly laughter that any child — any grown-up — ever hungered to hear. Great guffaws, beautifully breathless alto aw-awed-aws, sweet-rill hosannahs, and all of it amplified. Yet, the knot of a dozen or so kids stays silent. Not a single child laughs with Sal and except for a shaky giggle or two no one attempts to laugh at her. Facing a performer so pure and immense, the children clamp their own mouths. Then they feel what they do when nearing the crest of the Thriller's first hill: inching through their spines is a shallow shiver of fear.

Even the youngest in the group of kids has a look of horror. He is watching a figure that seems to be laughing, but the smile is frozen. The sounds tumbling out of her mechanical lips belong to someone real or, what is more likely, to someone who at one time was real. The older children milling before the glass hazard a few guesses, throwing out names of dead or long-gone female celebrities whose auras still loom large enough to do something as odd as this: give their laughter away to a giant amusement park doll. Could it be the sound of that Sophie Tucker — what was it their parents called her, again? The last? The last of the red-hot mamas? Could it be the chortling of Kate Smith, the one in the graying film clips who sang *O, Say Can You See* with a gutsy vibrato at baseball games, until something sad or mean or political happened to her? Could this be the secret giddiness of Mae West, who strutted a stage with a hand on her hip and smirked but didn't quite laugh, but who, alone and in private, would have let loose, doubled over with a case of the giggles, slapping her thighs at how she'd put one over on those poor saps again? Who was laughing in Euclid Beach Amusement Park, year after year? Who left her voice behind?

Sal leans back from her waist, her arms widen jerkily, helpless to stop their rise into the air. Her palms show themselves to the crowd — open, vulnerable, not greedy — and out the human music rolls. Late at night, into dawn, through daylight, through spats of rain and snow, Laughing Sal will never stop laughing. Sal standing still? Without voice and sound? Sal is mechanical; with a switch and a current, with tape spools inside her, she reels backward, and goes on and on and on and on.

(REEL ONE, SIDE A)

The first voice ever recorded and reproduced was Thomas Alva Edison's. What did he think to say for posterity? "Mary had a little lamb. Its fleece was white as snow." Before Edison recited the opening of a nursery rhyme, every other voice in history, no matter how powerful the speaker or crucial the message, faded after the instant of striking the air. It was a given that voices, like life, flew forward too fast. Voices stirred, said their piece, and in the swoop of a second — to borrow a Euclid Beach Park analogy — whee! Thriller! Laugh in the Dark! Over the Falls!

Heard in their own time and not again: the individual voices of Alexander, Caesar, Cleopatra, Catherine, Napoleon. Lost in their immediate embrace: the vocal tones and endearments of Solomon, David, Jonathan, Ruth, Naomi. Not again heard as a measure of evidence: the sagacious pronouncements of Abraham, Buddha, the Delphic Oracles, Lao-tzu, Jesus, Muhammad. Silent as print: the corridor chattering of Louis XIV, Isabella, Elizabeth I, Cornwall, Franklin, Washington, Adams, Lincoln. Not saved: one cry in particular, or a choir of seven, or the babble of thousands. Out of the swollen pleas of those being driven from second Jerusalem, from the rich valley beneath smoldering Vesuvius, from the tribal lands of the North American plains, from the battlefields scouring every century before the megaburst steel of the twentieth, no sound remains.

In the late 1800s, Thomas Alva Edison, leaning forward into the next turn, spoke clearly. His voice jiggled a tiny ball-pointed stick that responded by denting a sheet of tin foil molded around a grooved metal cylinder. A few moments later when the cylinder was hand-cranked, Edison's slow tones tumbled into the air and Mary's little lamb romped off in a far pasture. For the first time, a man was separated from the production of his own voice. He could hear its sound reproduced not as the waning last syllables of an echo but preserved whole — his voice whole again — from start to finish, as if just leaving his lips. He could turn and walk away, it would remain where he had left it. His body might wither or grow, but his voice, housed in the dashes, dents, and dots of a foreign object, would not change an iota. Even after his death, it could ring out.

That innocently, with nursery rhyme, tinfoil, and drum, time's harsh claim on our voices ended. At the start, though, Edison's phonograph was no less a source of entertainment than was any amusement park ride. The machines were rented out to traveling salesmen who acted like sideshow barkers to generate excitement. At each stop on the circuit, the public eagerly lined up to experience a full evening's thrills of the touted "captured voices" sneezing, sighing, talking animatedly in English and foreign languages, even mooing, cawing, hissing, and bleating baa-baa. A few of these auditory roller coasters reportedly pulled in two thousand dollars a week, an immense sum back then. Inevitably the novelty wore off. Part of the public's declining interest would have been due to the routine mechanical disruptions: the thin wrappings rubbed away after a few revolutions and the device was skittish to operate. These physical difficulties underscored a feeling that although "captured voices" might be independent of the human body, they yet were subject to the diminishments of time.

The other part? The public hungered for a measure of autonomy and control over the recording process. People were still materially distanced from producing any voice other than their own. They must have wearied of applauding the device's rudely calculated displays: barnyard soliloquies, throat clear-ings, coughing. As Samuel Johnson quipped snidely in a differ-ent context (he was commenting about the attention then be-ing given to the new female preachers): "It is like a dog's walking on its hinder legs. It is not that it is done well; but you are surprised to find it done at all."

In the end, the selection of voices pulled around the cylinder didn't sustain allegiance because they were composed of the thinnest of foils: they were made for surprise. They sent out sound, it is true, but they did not fully speak to their listeners. They weren't those voices that would take listeners to the bright edge, and bring them back.

(REEL THREE, SIDE A)

"Oh, the light's blinking now — it's started, it's turning inside. Nonny, hurry!"

Throat-clearing noises; the foom of an exhalation directed into the microphone's knobby screened head. Lurching tone; blurts loudly; the words running together as one, as if what she has to say will have to travel fast and far: "Iloveyou."

Laughter. "No, say something else. Be natural. You can tell a story. I'm ready; try again now."

Foom. "Iloveyou."

"Nonny!"

"Iloveyou."

"Non!"

"Iloveyou."

"Robert, where are you? Come and help me convince Nonny that she has to say something else for the machine. She's like a record that skips. Nonny's really stuck. Hey, Rob?"

Pause button. Click. Dead space.

Click on. No central voice, no narrator, no reporter. As if

we've entered a forest or wood, just rustlings and indistinct scamperings of scurry and breath. Underbrush crackles. Branches, leaves whisper. Wind, weightless, barely moves. Silence. Distance. Floating faint, muttered phrases. Nothing close to decipherable. Then: laughter from young boys. Chair scrapings. Clink and bright clatter. From another place Dad calling, "When's dinner ready, Phyllis?"

Mom's voice comes in so smoothly from the side it seems to arc in the same breath as it fades. "Soon," she says. "It won't be long, Gene." For some moments, all sound stills, muffled as if in a room stuffed with too much air. Then: footsteps. Toe- and heel-strikes moving closer. Pause button. Click.

The tape hitches, snags.

Reverse button. Speed as high whine. Whee!

Pause button. The tape flexes and stops. The loops tighten in opposite directions, resume spinning.

Rising to the surface as if breaking upward through currents, Robby sings forth, his voice cracking with adolescence, two scales cleared by joy: "We've got spaghetti. Houston, we have liftoff. Everyone, come and get it!"

The few times I've asked friends what they'd like to say about tape recorders, I've received an astounding reply: each mentions being the sole child in the family who received a recorder as a birthday or holiday present. Only Donna was given a tape recorder. Only Lee. Only Martin. Apparently, no sibling had one, nor did any cousin. Yet whomever I've thought to ask: bingo, the kid with the microphone. Maybe this says something about the friends I've chosen. More likely it speaks to an intimate relationship people want to claim: we believe that at some early point we were given a gift, the ability to control — to record and preserve — the voices we love. And we adjust our memories in many different ways, to allow the reverberation.

My first tape recorder was a small but clunky affair, about the size of a complete, boxed set of fancy bond stationery. I, too, recall it coming to me as a gift. I believe that I requested it from my parents when I was fourteen or fifteen. By then I would have already possessed what we then called a "portable" transistor radio to slip inside a canvas tote bag. On sweltering summer afternoons, my friends and I would walk the mile or so to Thornton Park's public pool. We'd stretch out in bright two-piece bathing suits on big towels laid atop the concrete, everyone's black transistor radio tinnily tuneful with the same rock and roll: the British invasion of mop-top Beatles, the African click-language of Miriam Makeba, California's nice surfer Beach Boys, Detroit's churning heat wave of Martha Reeves and the Vandellas, or the amber honey harmonies of Tammi Terrell and Marvin Gaye. Pop music's democracy of everywhere, brought right to us. We balanced little plastic spoons over our eyes so the thin skin of our lids wouldn't burn, and seeing only red from the sun through our curved, apportioned dark, blindly laughed, blindly listened and sang, blindly and happily baked and rocked. So carefree! We stretched full-length beneath the rays, basking in the flood of sound from the small devices placed on the edge of our towels. Transistor radios were definitely amusing, summertime things.

It would have been around this time that I started avoiding the high diving board. I'd climb the wet metal steps up to Thornton Park's highest platform, bounce on the sandpaper-rough edge, and freeze, even though I'd been executing back flips, jackknives, and swan and straight dives from that kind of a height for a couple of years. Perhaps I'd ended the previous summer with the shock of a belly-slam, where the body hits the water at the wrong angle and the peaky sharp surface punishes you for it. But every summer brought plenty of belly-slams; I'd always come up from them sputtering and grinning.

Suddenly, though, I did not want to seek another free ride downward through space. The untethered drop. The knowledge that by springing off from that flexible board, I could aim, and miss. Or maybe, now that I think of it, I was sixteen then, the summer when I got frightened about diving — which would make it about eight months after my grandfather died. I can't be sure, because it was just another part of everything that seemed to be changing, but my strongest sense of this theory is to stamp it with the word: yes. Yes, without record. The transistor radios playing from the damp towels, and one body poised, arms over head, at the edge, gleaming in the bright sun, and then, unlike being strapped in and set on a track, just plunging.

For the life of me, it seems that these three disparate things — high-board diving, the constant stream from transistor radios, and Papa's death from a heart attack the autumn preceding — were crucial to my being given a tape recorder, a gift I am certain that I asked to receive, because somehow I understood I was already too late to grab hold of a voice that I loved. A radio is important for what in the present flows through it. A recorder for what from the present it captures and stops. When you listen to a tape, you are listening to time. Push *record now* and, as with a camera, you are making a memory; you seize sound for the future. My sense is that at sixteen I would have been aware of death, finally, as tangible. One leap away from the adolescent's eternal present, from a child's storied innocence and fidelity. One free-form leap. One swoop. One splash. Just that. A song, a voice, a life in the air. And no more.

"I'd like a tape recorder for my birthday, I think. I'd like to try and interview everyone."

In fits and starts, with breaks that sometimes lasted years, I set the spools reeling. I didn't announce my true intentions in tap-

43

ing, not even to myself, but I went after my subjects with a mix of abashed dedication and supreme nonchalance: Nonny, Mom, Dad, Rob, Cliff, Dan; my first boyfriends, and my first girlfriends, one way or another I captured their voices. The machines became progressively trimmer and lighter — each recorder that much more portable, more sensitive to retrieving a side sigh or flutter, each more advanced. The tapes that snapped out of them were not the product of professional polish, but of the silent enthusiasms of love. Like love they were not stacked in canonical order. Instead, they lay jumbled together in bags and rubber-banded shoe boxes, wedged one by one into back cupboards; some sat right in plain view, silent and unmoved — if dusted — for years.

(REEL EIGHT, SIDE B)

"Hey, it's going around. Okay. Okay, Robert, would you mind telling me what you did today?"

"That's not the most fascinating question to start out with, you know."

"You mean that you had a boring day?"

"I didn't say that."

"Was your day interesting, then?"

"This is ridiculous, Marcie. We both have better things to do."

"We do not. What are you saying? Oh, wait, I bet you have homework. What is social studies, can you explain it? The study of in-groups and cocktail parties?"

"I haven't taken social studies since eighth grade."

"Then, say something in Latin and I'll leave you alone. Say: *Semper ubi sub ubi.* I know it's silly; it's just the kind of a joke — Always wear underwear — that we won't remember when we get old. Say it. How else can we know what we liked as kids? So, will you? Direct your voice into the microphone, please."

"I can't believe you."

"Hah! Yes, you can."

"You're right, unfortunately I can. But I can't, too. Not under it all."

"Robert, stay. At least say: 'Hello, this is Marcie's nice, smart brother talking to you from the way-ago year of 1968, the spring of her junior year in high school, when she finally matched me and got all A's.' Would you say that, please, and speak up? I'd really like to have you talking.

"Rob?"

My first long project, and the only one I planned much beforehand, was the five sides of tape (each cassette an hour and a half in length) that I recorded with Nonny in 1977, when she was seventy-six and I was twenty-six. I wanted to have her stories, told in her own voice and in her own way. Over a mix of three mornings and afternoons we sat down at the vinyl-topped card table in the yellow den of her third-floor apartment outside of Cleveland. It was summer, and very warm. On the tape you can hear traffic whisking beneath the open window, linked rapid-transit cars clacking along the tracks on Van Aken Boulevard, the occasional bleating bap of a horn; you can catch the smooth scrape and clink of spoons as we ate our sweet scoops of vanilla and lemon sherbert from Nonny's flowery European bowls; you can hear the air conditioner's fan whirring in the den's other window. On the tape you can hear: we sat close, and ate slowly, and chatted. Nonny leaned forward. She spoke into the microphone. She began the tape by pronouncing excessively carefully, as if trying to communicate with somebody who had to read lips, a litany of foreign names: Szacsur, her small village in Hungary/Czechoslovakia; you should say it like "such-oor"; Nagymihály, Papa's little bit bigger village; you say it so it sounds like "nudge-me-high"; her father's name: Isadore Polak; her mother's name: Freida Polak; her maternal grandmother, the last name: Dagenstein, and she spoke "high Deutsche" — proper formal German — and she held herself erect. Oh, when she went to live with this grandmother while she attended gymnasium — this was what they called the high school — she was unhappy. This grandmother was too strict, too stern. Don't do this, she would say, don't do that. Don't stay out late, don't dawdle, you come right home. One day, well, she decided enough was enough, she should go to America. Why? Because the family had to eat. Her father, Isadore, had died of influenza around the time of the Great War. After that, life was tough. All over Europe, it was the same. No one had enough, no one had what to eat. She decided that she would go to America and find work, like her father had done in the early years, so she could send money back to her mother and her five sisters. Well, her sisters' names were: Sarain ("Sarah"), Margite, Ilone ("Ee-lone"), Irain, Etel (Ethel). . . .

In America, see, life was different. Better. And of course she met Papa. She met him one night, all of them just talking together in a big group of friends. The next morning, she opens the door of her brownstone tenement, to go to work in the factory where she had a job sewing buttons on spats, and who is waiting on the bottom step of the pavement? Harry Weiss. What's the big idea, she said. What are you doing here? I'm going to walk you to work, he said. So, they walked. And every morning after, she opened her door and there he was. That was the start, see?

On five sides of tape, we traveled all the way from phonetic pronunciations and genealogies to the give-and-take of casual conversation, from the self-consciousness of lineage to the utter naturalness and self-forgetfulness of live interaction. The final reel has Nonny confiding in low tones that she blames my first serious boyfriend for "ruining" me for other men, which is why she thinks I turned to women, and my horrified response, "Oh, Nonny, no! Don't blame Jack. Really, he had nothing to do with it. What you're thinking is not one bit how it was." All the while, spinning in the background is the summery world, filled with clattering tracks, streaks of traffic, whirring fans, spoon clink, ice-cream slurp. Talk, talk, talk. Five sides of two voices. Up the incline, and — with a swoop and a great crying whoop — quickly down. Circling from past history to the just-now moment. From fact to action. Nonny's voice vibrant, ringing with opinion and incident; mine, so easily and immediately inquisitive. Both voices riding together through five looping lengths of glittering tape. That was almost half my lifetime ago.

To go back, push: repeat.

You would think I'd play them. You'd think I would set them spinning, maybe once a year, or at least every now and then.

But when I think of getting out the recorder, something catches in my throat.

Six years after our taping, Nonny's memory deteriorated. Over the next few years, she began to forget little things: where she'd put her pocketbook, how to roll out the yeasty dough for kuchen; then she forgot bigger things: where she lived, all of our names (except for one, that of her daughter, our mother, Phyllis.) She believed once or twice that she was back in Szacsur, when the Russians were breaking down the door of her family's store again to ransack and rape. Inevitably, she had to yield. She had to give herself over — be taken over by the achronology of loss, the chaos illness that we term Alzheimer's disease. The scattershot horror, striking inside and out, of mind-blank.

But what I want to give voice to here is what happened when she heard one of the tapes again. This was when she was living in the Assisted Care facility. It was well before she went into a spartan shared room in the nursing home, and well before in that home, nearly mute, immobile, and almost entirely erased, she willed herself — in her last brave clear autonomous act — to stop eating, so she might exit what, one afternoon, she termed, in a sudden burst of clarity, hell. ("Do you want me to be in hell?" she'd demanded, pulling back from the spoon of soft food I'd been holding to her lips. "Well, this is hell.") My parents had told me over the phone how they'd picked her up from Assisted Care so they could spend the day together at their condo; at one point, after dinner, they stuck into their audio system a copy of one of the tapes I'd made. Mom settled her frail mother on the couch, tucking the knitted afghan about her. Dad pushed the play button and adjusted the volume. The clinking of spoons. The whirring fan blades. Our two voices speaking, easy with the back and forth. Nonny listened politely and pleasantly enough, they told me. Then, when the cartridge's first side clicked to shift to the second, she cocked her head. With a slight smile, she said quietly, "You know, one day I'd like to meet that person."

(REEL FIFTEEN, SIDE A)

It wasn't I who ended up wielding a recorder and microphone on a regular basis, but Rob. He became a producer of short documentaries. Just as he had read widely and classically as a boy, easily bounding continents and cultures, so he ranged the globe in the present tense when he went to work first for public

48

television's *The MacNeil-Lehrer Report* and then for the news division at CBS—for *West 57th* and *48 Hours*. His tasks as producer were varied and complex. Most people's idea of what a producer does comes from the movies; film producers are portrayed as glam guys, suits (Prada or Armani) with deep pockets, princes of purse strings. Television news producers, however, have little to do with raising funds or counting profits. Rather, in TV news, the producers *are* the show, they *make* it, even if they rarely pop up on the screen.

Rob, for example, would search out the stories he might want to cover (a passenger jet that dropped a thousand feet through the air, then righted itself before hitting the ground; a fundamentalist coup percolating in post-Shah Iran; an East European diplomat robbed of a suspiciously heavy briefcase and murdered while crossing a bridge into his own country; family members in conservative Orange County, California, living with AIDS); then he'd track down and briefly interview those people involved. Back in his hotel room or in his office in New York, he'd replay his tapes and jot notes. He'd interview others. He'd schedule the shoot after figuring its logistics: on this date, in this location, with such and such a person, over so many hours. On location, my brother would speak to the reporter whose likable face would fill the sweet spot in the camera lens and he'd hand over the list of questions he'd written, culled from the tapes. It was a list in set order, finely tuned, with wording if not formal, then a hairbreadth shy of colloquial. Then Rob would choose a backdrop—a sun-splashed house wall, a distant river—and he'd say solicitously to the reporter, "Let's position you over there," and to the interviewee, "I think you'll be comfortable right *here*." His tones were as gracious and welcoming as those of a dinner host, and, like a host, he had command of everyone's placement. He would cue the operator of the video camera, nod at the earphone-wearing operator of the miked boom and audio equipment, and: "Stand by! Roll sound!"

Said the reporter, addressing the stranger seated not two feet away, "When did you first learn about . . . ?"

The list in the reporter's hand just out of view was Rob's voice. His curiosity, his intonation, his intent of focus. The reporter leaned forward, and settled back. The same gestures of intense interest, again and again. The videotape whirled. The audio dials trembled. Later, from their side of the glass, remote controls for TV or VCR in their hands, others would watch the action, a seamless edit of give-and-take. They did not consider that out of the reporter's mouth was coming anyone else's voice but his or her own. Why would they?

Honestly, I wouldn't have considered such a proposition either, until I went on location with Rob. I was the first in the family to observe him in action. He'd invited me to join him, a prospect I'd never considered, since his work was, after all, demanding, not a source for others' vacations. I'd just finished working on my third novel, the four-year-long project that I hoped would result in my first published book, and I was at loose ends while my agent (ah, I'd gotten an agent!) sent the manuscript to publishers. In part, Rob asked me to come visit him because he knew I was floating, and because Ron, his funny, loving partner of ten years, had just, at age thirty-one, received a firm diagnosis for the fearsome chills and night sweats, the blue welts on his back, the fits of coughing and dry mouth. Ron was not ill enough then for Robert to stop working and stay home to tend to him — and Rob was not going overseas for ten days in the summer of 1987 because he needed an escape from the diagnosis that Ron was HIV-positive. He asked me to be with him because he wanted to speak without a sheet of glass between us. He felt healthy and energetic, but he suspected that time might be getting short. The world was spinning. The ride through it was *now*. It couldn't be put off much longer. Robert was nearing the top of the first hill. Soon the wind could be roaring from his mouth.

"Why don't you visit me while I'm working on location," he asked, phoning from New York.

"Really?" I said, pleased.

"Sure. You can fly over a few days after I get to Munich. I have a lot to prepare at the beginning, so I'll be no fun to be around then, but the rest of the filming should be fascinating. After the shoot, we can take a train across the border to Italy. We can hike in the Dolomites — I've always wanted to do that. The northern Alps are breathtaking. We can hang out for a couple more days and enjoy ourselves. Then we'll go to Milan and from there you can fly back to Boston and I'll go back to New York to begin work on the edits. We've never done this before, have we?"

"Hold on. You're asking me to meet you in Germany?"

"Exactly." Static buzzed through the line. "You'll come to Munich."

"Munich," I said flatly.

He explained how he was shooting a story centered on the first awarding of the Scholl Prize, named for the German brother and sister who had belonged to the White Rose, the anti-Nazi student group in World War II. Hans was a medical student and Sophie had just begun her studies in art at the same university. They were very close, Rob said, Hans and Sophie. The twelve or so members managed to distribute three mimeographed flyers stating their opposition to Hitler's regime before four of them were caught. Two of those arrested were the Scholls. Throughout their interrogation and imprisonment not one member spoke against the group's actions. Along with their philosophy professor, all were executed by guillotine.

Rob said he'd gone over earlier to talk with Hans and Sophie's sister. He'd also interviewed Anya Rosmus, the first recipient of the prize, for her work as a student uncovering records that detailed her hometown's pro-Nazi activities during the war. It was a past that her neighbors vociferously, at times violently, denied. Despite threats, Rosmus wouldn't be budged. And she was raising her two children where she'd grown up.

"I've scheduled us to tape in Munich for six days, plus the day when we'll have to head out to Passau to interview Anya. Passau is situated above the Danube, very medieval, near the eastern border. It's all timbers and stone. You should be there. What do you think?"

"I'm not sure."

"Come on, what are you thinking? Is it because of Rebecca that you're hesitating?" he said. "Because the relationship is still new? What, five months? Six?"

"No, I'm certain she'd tell me to go. She loves travel herself. She'd understand. And then, she'd want me to have this chance, you know, to be with you. I'm not worried that way. We're going to be together a long, long time, I think."

"Then what is it?"

"I'm not sure," I said again. "I don't know." I could hardly squeeze the words out. "In any case, it sounds as if you've already decided what's happening. You told it to me like you've got everything planned."

"I was just talking off the top of my head." Rob laughed then, a little throatily. "Anyway, it's the crew I've scheduled. Not you. Will you consider it?"

I wanted to agree. I wanted very much to be with him. Yet he was asking me to travel through the one country I hoped never to visit. The source of the silences in our grandmother's stories. The source of her blank, bitter silence when, too young to understand, we would lean against her from either side and ask, "But what happened to your mother and sisters after you left them in Hungary, Nonny? If they stayed, then how can your family be gone now? Where did they go? Where did Papa's family go?"

"Marcie," Robert said, breaking in over the phone. His tone quiet. "These are the few people who resisted. These are the fighters."

Another part: it is a great gift, you know, for a brother and sister to travel past their childhoods as adults who enjoy one another.

My flight over was trackless and moonless and once or twice, catching a sluicing current, stomach-dropping. The ocean was midnight. I had a three A.M. layover in London's Heathrow airport. There, my sole piece of luggage rolled down a chute, passed through two doors, and got lost. For the first two days in a disconcertingly sunny Munich, I wore Rob's shirt. The shoulders hung down nearly to my elbows, making my arms feel even more exposed than if they'd been capped with my own shorter short sleeves. It was from inside my brother's borrowed shirt that I stood back on street corners and cordoned-off rooms to watch him. How calmly he went about the difficult business of bringing sense to so much vocal tilting and spilling. As questions about procedure and protocol flurried toward him, he dealt with each in its turn, from setting up equipment to negotiating the autobahns to translating languages. His decisions were swift, yet came across as unhurried. I saw some of our grandfather's mannerisms in Robert's, but something steely in him too that seemed all his own.

While I stood with small groups of German onlookers who whispered among themselves about what it might be that the Americans were so busy recording, it struck me with great force that I worked alone. Writing sets you on a route that, no matter how satisfying, is almost unutterably solitary. Film, however, is a communal enterprise. The gravitational core of this particular five-member group? A good-looking, olive-skinned, dark-eyed man in a crew neck sweater and chinos, not tall, not short, armed with tape recorder, clipboard, and an ever-increasing number of densely filled pages of notes. In a very material sense he was *producing:* moving a community to this place and that, bringing speakers forward, directing a stream of isolated words and images into coherence, and onto the same loop. I could see how much he enjoyed managing the reciprocal tensions of collaboration. Was that what I was to witness? Back in the circle of family, hadn't he been (and wasn't he still on most visits?) the one who kept himself off to the side, purposely absorbed in a task, the one who only briefly raised his eyes — to meet my long gaze? Now he looked up amid jangling cords and reels to find me, both of us glad. Here, in this place, this frightful source of vacancy.

Back in the old ornate Hotel Vier Jahreszeiten, in the small double room we shared, he would dial Ron, home in New York. How was he feeling? Were the meds helping? Which friends had he seen? Who else had stopped by? Rob stood at the desk before the heavy closed drapes, his back to me, shoulders rounded, leaning over the phone. Hunched like that, button-down shirt hanging untucked, he listened very quietly. He stood nearly still. On the other side of the door, I heard wheels, a clinking, rattling cart; the sound rumbling past out of nowhere. Then Ron said something, and Robert's shoulders lifted. Head tipping back, he straightened and laughed gleefully, with a full expense of breath. It was like watching someone who had been frozen take a sudden leap. He laughed again in open joy. Robert swiveled and held the receiver in front of his chest, tilting it through the air toward me.

"Hey," I called across the room. "Rob's being good, Ron." I aimed my words at my target, the black mouthpiece in my brother's hand. "He's good."

The cart outside rattling past, as farther away a small voice, so faint it was barely familiar, shouted in greeting.

(REEL SIX, SIDE B)

Behind the glass partition Sal is reeling way backward, throwing her palms above her head. With a sly, flushed smile, Robby leans close and cups a hand around Marcie's ear. Whatever he whispers makes her turn to him with a quick grin. Sal howls with laughter. Not quite in sync, brother and sister shuffle a few steps back from the glass. Have they had enough for now? Are they saying good-bye for the season? Small clouds of dust waft from the white rubber soles of their Keds. Cliffy and Danny, too, don't fight to stay. They are already listing toward sleep. All four children are wrung out by the battery of sensation: Loud! Quiet. Up! Down. Now! Then. Around! Around. Around! How vast Euclid Beach Park still seems. Rides clatter, spinning bodies against the sky. Arms wave from the speeding cars. Not quite visible yet is the moon, the great cut circle of time, as it moves in accord with the earth. The crowds press close, almost touching as they rush past, their skin radiating heat, their faces alert and sweaty, their mouths full of chatter; then like nothing they fade away.

Soon, there is nowhere to look back to. The children have fallen silent. I've let go of their hands. Alone, I pass beneath the park's huge iron archway and go forward. I can almost hear Sal. The sound of life escaping, yet eternally trapped. The tape will rewind. It unwinds. Such sound, such voice — all of it is laughter, beautiful and grotesque.

Dream Dialogues

Sounds have to be located in space, identified
by type, intensity, and other features. There
is a geographical quality to listening.
— DIANE ACKERMAN

I lie down and whether I will it or not, dreams possess me every night. Sometimes they linger past dawn, whispering endearments, whispering: Will you remember? Sometimes I do remember them later; more often, I don't. As someone who has slept and awakened in regular cycles during the Freudian, Jungian, feminist post-Freudian, and mechanistic REM/brain wave eras, and who has read of dream messages in the Bible (seven rich harvest years, Pharaoh, to be followed by the sorry bovines of seven lean ones), I both believe and wave away theories of how dreams make a difference.

It is now the year 2000, some five millennia past Joseph's saving prophesy in Egypt, one hundred and one years since Sigmund Freud published his mind-opening, emotions-keyed treatise, *The Interpretation of Dreams,* in German, and nearly fifty years since the discovery in a Chicago, Illinois, laboratory of a biological basis for dreams in REM sleep, where for brief intervals approximately ninety minutes apart, the eyes move rapidly as a reflex triggered by bursts of neural activity in the brain. We have been talking about dreams for as long as we've had them, stirring them like tea leaves in the bottom of a cup, parsing them like lines of dense poetry, measuring and weighing them, cutting them up. We fold them into boxes neatly labeled: spirit, mind, body. More, we haven't stopped arguing.

57

We argue about why dreams occur, what dreaming means, and who we really are. There is a lot at stake. We live in dual realities, the everyday world of outer experience with its corners, imprints, and bruises, and we live in the everynight world of flux and ungraspable inner experience.

We live in both. We are caught in both. We are changed by both. And if we can pretend to know what the daylight world is about, then it is not quite clear what goes on when our house walls cross into shadow and we close our eyes.

Each day we rise and look back at ourselves still lying abed, beings full of strangeness.

Look at yourself in your bed. You can see yourself lying quite still outside your own dream. *There,* under the sheets. Face blind to the ceiling, you lie on your back. Your lips quiver with a low moan. Inside your dream, you are racing. (Do you recall it, the heart pounding, the quick, happy shouts? Racing after X, you leapt the gray split-rail fence; on the other side, you scrambled to your feet, the high grasses rising about you, a dry sea glinting with sun. The blades rippling overhead as X ran farther, hidden, and you were swimming now, kicking, stroking in the shining wake X left behind for you like a road.) Yes, you see that you are lying outside a dream, swathed and silent beneath a white sheet, and you also recall that you were there within it (a world as real, as unquestionable, as anything is real and unquestionable). In that inner world you raised your head, calling with a cry so full it contained the pressure of deepest need— *Wait! Wait!*

Both your voices waking you.

A light sleeper, I wake as swiftly to thunder in the distance as I do to my partner's sigh. What sounds from outside has the power to rouse me. Rebecca, whose long body is distant from mine each night by a matter of inches, sleeps in a different country, a downy thick swaddled place, undisturbed by murmurs or passing storms. If I turn over beside her and mutter: *Are you awake now?* or, louder: *Give me part of the blanket,* the roll of vibration gets absorbed into her dream. At the most, my voice is a director's cue called from off set, changing the flow of events. But if Rebecca lets slip the mumbled scramble of a question, no matter how serene the breath it rides in on, it splits my dream open. Then I am up on an elbow, eyes opening fast to the dark. *What is it?* I demand of her form in the air. *What?*

Why are people hungry to learn if they dream in color? The question I am eager to ask is: Do you hear in your dreams? Do you recognize as particulars the sounds of wineglasses chiming and voices ringing out? Do you discern the high vocal split separating celebration from alarm? Or do you spend your nights reading lips? Watching the dumb show unfurl, do you take in grins, grimaces, flicks of the tongue, as visual aids translating words shaped *as if they can be heard* into the subtlety of words *seen as understood.* Sound is brain spark, and not truly sound—is that what you say? Or, is there someone whose voice you could state without equivocation: *Yes, I heard X in my dream. She spoke and I heard her. Her voice, and no one else's.*

My grandmother once told me how much she wanted my grandfather to come back in a dream. This was years after he'd died. Every day something happened—or nothing happened—that stung with one touch: how much she missed him. Passing the bright outdoor display window of a clothing store, say, she'd turn to ask for his comment, or she'd bend to retrieve the morning's *Plain Dealer* from the apartment's doormat and look back at the thud of a footfall in the hallway behind her. She wasn't silly about it. He wasn't coming back here again, she knew that; but the world made of spirit or mind might be different. Anna longed to hear the quiet rumble of Harry's voice. At night, she'd close her eyes so that he would visit. He did not.

Was it absurd or somehow sad to confess to such a hope? I don't think so. Dreams are often the first place anyone turns to communicate with those they have lost. Many of us do it, but keep what we wish for a secret. We barely admit, perhaps even to ourselves, that dreams offer a respite from the hard narrow edge of separation. After all, we are still arguing about the stuff they are made of. Yet, as we lie down, we agree that we might crack open the door to something that we do not understand and cannot control: the not-material, not-actual, a dream of our connection to a place beyond *this*.

I was stretched out on the living room rug, taking deep breaths to cut my apprehension. Although I knew what had to come next in the chapter, I somehow could not get myself up and at the desk to write it. Then, earlier than expected, Carly called on her cell phone. She was still north of Portland, driving south down through Maine. She had just dropped her eleven-year-old daughter off at overnight camp for the first time. She was supposed to be heading next to visit me, but she was weepy and wrung out from leaving her child, and the prospect of an additional five hours in the already close and cramped hatchback added to her sense of exhaustion. She wanted to beg off our original plans, suggesting for now an open-ended postponement. I understood, but wasn't shy expressing my disappointment. We'd known each other for twenty-seven years, though that hardly seemed possible, and to our chagrin hadn't managed to see each other for the last two. In the next month she and her two children were going to move overseas. I pointed out that given the move, we had no other time to meet up. Now or never, kiddo, I said. Too quickly she agreed that I was right. It felt terrible to think about changing things, she said. I waited. With an edge to my tone I said, Well? Then more angrily: Well, is that it for us? Carly was driving into a tunnel of trees that closed in on her in a single gulp, the darkness so dense with needles no branches were visible. "I don't know where I'm going," she said. "Wait, Marcie, okay?" I could hear her in her small car, the wind a rush past the window, then without fanfare or warning, static cut us off.

When my end of the line rang some twenty minutes later, she was speeding through a new zone, and the cell's connection was clear. The break seemed to have swept away any old expectations. We both laughed, talking over each other's "Hey, you still there?" As for apologies and recriminations, they were behind in the twisting claustrophobia of the forest. After the tunnel, the expanse before her now, Carly said, sounding startled, was almost blinding. It was strange how wide and bright it was just on the other side.

"Let me ask you something."

"Okay."

"Has Lauren ever come back in a dream?" Phone to my ear, I settled against the couch, as if this was really at the heart of what we'd been talking about just before the disconnect, her sister's death at thirty-three from cancer. Lauren, vivacious, gloriously ambitious, and self-assured, died eight years after Carly and I met during our senior year of college in Boston. She died in the sole stretch when Carly and I were in hiatus, determinedly establishing our young adult lives in two different cities.

"Oh, yes," she said eagerly. "Yes, many times."

I sat up. "Really? And she spoke to you?"

The rush of the wind lessened. She was closing up the windows in the car. "Oh, yes." Carly sounded happy.

"Did her voice sound like you remembered? Could you recognize it?"

"Of course I could! I know the sound of my sister's voice."

"You don't think it was something other than — ?"

"We were talking," Carly said. "And I asked her what it felt like to die. She said, 'I'll show you.'"

How silly of me to be holding my breath.

Carly went on, "I had the sensation of rising. I was floating upward and I felt just ecstatic. That was the feeling, ecstatic. It was beautiful. I've never felt afraid again. I truly have not."

To my dismay I found myself smiling. I had the wry slight smile of the intellectual. I was thinking: Well, this was how she convinced herself that her sister hadn't suffered when she passed from life into death. Through the medium of dream, Carly spoke to herself about her fears. In using dream psychology's imagistic puns, Carly allowed herself to "rise above" her fears for her sister and for herself. She felt light, free of the weight that bound her to this earth, the earth in which our bodies get buried. Or in biologically defined terms, despite what she believed she had *heard* in those moments — her sister's own voice, a sister's generosity given to her, the younger sibling — it was well-timed neural activity. REM, rapid eye movement and, let's say, rapid ear movement, too — brain bursts of image and auditory memory; the vestibular system adding a sensation of floating. Lauren was a mix of chemical energies. Dreams, an envelope with a message inside? Dreams a gift of connection of life and sound?

"What was interesting," my friend said, still confiding, "is that I was having another dream at the time, and Lauren interrupted it."

"Ah," I said neutrally.

She laughed in a kind of release. "I can't even remember that one now. When I woke up, I couldn't either—I mean, who cared? It was only a nothing dream—you know, just a dream. Then Lauren barged into it. It was like she'd come in from somewhere else and knew that she had to break through all this junk that I was just sleeping through to give me the chance to ask her my question." With a laugh, she lowered her voice. "It's really good to finally talk about this. You know, it's the kind of thing that happens inside and it means so much, but you feel maybe a little queasy about admitting it to anyone else. You feel silly."

"Yeah," I said, playing with the cord, tugging it toward me in a tense line away from the oblong body of the phone. "You do. That's how you feel."

Any one-hundred-bucks analyst could parse my last sentences and find hiding in them ambiguity, deflection, denial, and projection of the Self's scary shadow onto the Other.

Translation: I was making Carly, who had spoken to me in open relief and without a shred of protective self-deprecation, bear the weight for my uneasiness over what I knew to be my own experience, the very experience I hoped outwardly to embrace and proclaim. Expensively educated, Western in orientation, living in a sophisticated East Coast city, I was embarrassed to say aloud or in writing what might sound—oh, I'll use my friend's word—"silly," then add to it my own phrase, skewed ironically between quotation marks, "New Agey." Yet, the dirtiness I felt as I smiled, reasoning away Carly's dream and the meaning it held for her, fell back on me doubled. Tethered to a cord in the living room as my friend sped through bright air, I'd used reason to deny myself the exhilaration of my own dreams. And, more, the private understanding I knew to be mine. That isn't an argument based on reason. It's based on something else, something small.

Silly.

How do you think of dreams?

A lifetime in a breath. A globe of light, spun. A party where the guests come to mingle and disappear. With an upsie-daisy legs wave in the air. Bodies take flight. There goes yours.

Sometimes you dread dreams as much as you seek them. Unpredictable. Incomprehensible.

I've had only two dreams of Robert since he died. The first came quickly. For some seconds it spilled into the darkness of April 11, 1995, exactly one month after Rob passed in the long hour, predawn, of March 11. Still, marking time is not the point here. In dreams, as in death, time is not linear. Time is the matter of breath.

In this first dream, I come back to my house to find it vandalized. I enter my study. Papers are strewn all over — everywhere, there is paper in shreds. Slips of paper on the floor, and covering the desktop. Panicked, I wrench open the desk's long middle drawer, sure the thief has stolen my checkbook. If he has, then he's already forged my signature, and taken that, too. I rummage through the drawer and, to my surprise, find the checkbook. But lying next to it is something I didn't expect. Something I did not know I even possessed. A photo of my smiling, thirtyish, healthy brother, riding in a car, the window rolled down behind him. Robert's face is partway turned toward the camera. He is caught, mid-word. His brown hair is wind-tugged off his brow. Behind, framed in the opened window and by the automobile's dark interior, is the streetscape. The buildings are blurred. So, given the angle and interior shadows, the picture was snapped from the driver's position and taken while moving. Taken in transit. I stare down at the image of Robert's grinning, talkative face. And can't move. "Rob!" the shout echoes. "Rob!" I am crying his name, yet at the same time I cry it, I hear it double back to me as this: "Thief!"

Rob.

Taken.

Silenced.

Gone.

The dream, coming at the start of a long process of mourning, held only my voice. That was *all* that I heard, and it *was* a nightmare. The stillness of Robert's features, his accessibility to me only in an image, his logical silence, all that said: death. And the isolation I felt as I awoke, the horror of the emptiness I was left with, permeated the morning's own silence. It was a silence that I felt (more than heard) surrounding me through the long grief that followed, when I could not seem to find my own voice in life or on the page. I could not make my own way into sound. A dry time, full of sorrow.

It took three more years — again, and perhaps you will find this unbelievable, precisely to the night — for my brother to return in a dream. This time, he was present in full. He was moving. More, he was singing. Rob's voice had always possessed the smooth energy of joy and so it did now. Robert was shining with pleasure, his arms wide, his eyes dark. He was climbing easily up a wooded slope toward me. He was thin and morphing back and forth from a face gaunt with the last days of his illness and his earlier face, full of rich health. I felt as if my chest would burst from the inside out, I was so happy to see him. I knew that he was dead, and I knew that I was dreaming, but I could hear him, and I was astonished, and I wanted that melody — a sweetness complete and free of lyrics — to go on and on.

I asked him what he was doing here. He said he was looking for a house, he needed to find a house. He did not say home but house — so I knew that he was not searching for the deep place where he would always dwell, but a temporary place where he might rest and be sheltered. Then I noticed that our parents were visible behind him, way down in the woods; they were getting out of some kind of van; they came up the hill; their movements were unrushed and light. Cliff and Dan appeared, too, and came up with our parents to surround Rob. They were all laughing. I heard their voices given to joy. But my focus was on Robert. He was central.

It was such a wonderful dream, even with the knowledge that it *was* a dream, that when I awoke, I told it to Rebecca, keeping my eyes still closed, for though I could no longer see it, I was not yet ready to become part of this world. For days afterward, I was imbued with happiness. I had heard my brother Rob singing to me.

I haven't heard him since. But I heard his voice as song in a place that cannot be destroyed.

In the end: I take my stand in meaning. Dreams speak and dreams mean. Any other answer lies not between the poles of either/or, but along the bridge of and.

Here I Am

I had heard of you by the hearing of the ear,
but now my eye sees you.

—JOB 42:5

I have never sung the following words, but on my brother's video I have heard others singing them; they are part of a language I do not speak: *"Kol ha'olam kulo gesher tzar me'od/ V'ha'ikar lo lefa-ched klal."*

"The world is just a narrow bridge," the congregation sings in Hebrew, their faces turned to the front where the podium is empty, "and the most important thing is not to fear at all." At this point, I recognize the top of my brother's head moving into the frame. Though I'd inserted the tape, I feel anxious about seeing him again. I know that he will reappear on the screen as he looked then, his face will be ill and scarred. My thumb bends at its single joint, poised atop the remote's stop button. But it seems that Rob has decided not to stand; he stays hidden behind the podium. Or perhaps the video camera, shaking and inexpertly wielded, has tilted just enough to sink my view.

The words the rabbi translated moments before into English reverberate as the congregation sings. Their voices are heartfelt and uneven. A narrow bridge. I can't listen to this. Pointing the remote, I hit the stop button. The twenty-five-inch television screen shoots full of static, then mutes via remote zap-zap. The dark square of glass crackles. I am thinking: The moments when we near the other end of the span must be among the most challenging. Everyone trembles on the approach. Too ill, too weary, some might cry, "I can't go on!" but, like Beckett's

67

great small characters Vladimir and Estragon, in the next breath, they will also announce, "I'll go on." Taking leave of the bridge happens to everyone. Yet not one of us truly sees what lies ahead next.

I once asked Robert if he was afraid. He told me that he wasn't — he said that he truly was not. "Rob, I'm afraid," I said. Robert said nothing. He was propped up against pillows, one eye covered over with gauze and bandages, the other eye open to me. Then he nodded. "I know you are, Marcie," he said quietly.

Robert started walking across the bridge all of a sudden more quickly than I. He tried turning back at the middle of the arc, and could not. The rule of the elder's protective watchfulness superceded by plague and illness. I could not grab hold of the tail of his shirt, tugging him back as I would have if he were still a small boy running heedless of danger into a busy street.

The world is a narrow bridge and the point is not to be afraid. I was afraid, though, watching him. Afraid, as I shouted for him. As I went after him, the distance between the two of us increasing with each stride or slide. At some point, the world split into multiple spans and Rob stood on one sweeping off in a direction that I couldn't follow. He was moving along an arc that seemed to me abruptly short yet was primed to take him somewhere much farther.

The label on the black plastic video box reads: "Rob Hershman, *Maggid* Ordination, December 11, 1994." Inside lay the videotape of a celebration driven to deadline by the human desire to say aloud and in public the same words that one dreads he or she will have to say later, when the recipient is no longer alive to receive them. The tapes were made as tokens of witness for those of us who could not travel to the ceremony in Los Angeles, the city where Robert moved in late 1992, three years after Ron's death, and a year and a half after meeting Gary, who as his life partner would make a new home with him.

Atop the videocassette was a note penned in blue ink in my brother's surprisingly crabbed handwriting. "Here's the tape of my *maggid* ceremony — all shot atop my friend Louise's 7-month pregnant tummy. How's that for life-affirming?" The padded mailer I'd ripped open also held a typed transcript of the speech — a speech that we read aloud now, paragraph by paragraph, at the Passover table at the point in the Seder related to the frightened Jews' exodus from Pharaoh's Egypt. It seems right to speak Robert's words then, when the table is full of plates and food, and history crowds in with nearly unimaginable hardships and journeys. It seems right to add my brother's words to the Seder's layered traditions because rituals must encounter the present as well as the past. To be alive, to move across, rituals must not be enacted as if their meaning just stopped, preserved in year A or at juncture C. Rituals, like life, must be renewed so that they can renew.

Until Rob's own ordination, I hadn't heard of the ceremony. In fact, the ritual is new, embraced by the more mystical Jews to whom Rob gravitated. The term, *maggid,* is spun from the source word meaning: "to tell it." A *maggid* is an individual who, while not a rabbi, is revered as a learned storyteller and teacher in the community. Essentially, a *maggid*'s job is to wake others up. The ordination ceremony honors the presence of a special voice. In particular, on December 11, 1994, in a community guided by Rabbis Jonathan Omer-Man and Judith Halevy, this new ritual honored Rob's voice and the urgency of the experience that kept deepening his message.

I'd tried to play the video all the way through only once before. That attempt came not long after the package arrived, in the first cold months of 1995. I recall Rebecca sitting on the wool rug beside me, her arm resting against mine. I faced the television screen not with stirrings of curiosity or joy, but a sense of gloom. I feared what was on the way. To see Robert as a gaunt image on videotape when I knew that in California, a continent distant, he awoke each day physically more drained than he appeared on this memento's projection? I could hardly listen to what he was saying as image filled the screen, so anxious was I to see and measure how ill — or how well — he looked. I could, however, focus easily on the written transcript of his speech, could by reading his words in their lines on a page hear Rob's strongest voice in my head, could in my mind's eye imagine him gesturing, his face shining. But I did not like the bridge upon which the videotape so implacably, startlingly, set us: one at either end, three thousand miles between us, and endlessness visible next.

A narrow bridge and the important thing? The remote is a black oblong with buttons up and down its front like the brass on a soldier's uniform. Now, for the second time in five years, I raise my hand and point: *there,* in the hope of moving across. The invisible eye winks. Fast-forward.

"We are in the denouement of the story of Joseph," my brother's voice says, from the direction of the screen. My head is down, but I know just where he is; he is picking up the ceremony just where I want him to, about to speak the same text of the transcript we read from at Passover. This will be where he interprets a story I used to hear without truly understanding it. But on tape, a new *maggid* is prepared to "tell it." His voice sounds reedy — strained with ill health, but determined to persevere. "You'll remember that Joseph is the second youngest of the patriarch Jacob's eleven sons, and the eldest of his beloved wife Rachel. He is his father's favorite and a pretty grandiose kid. Remember the coat of many colors and the dreams about his elder brothers bowing down to him?" he says. "The brothers finally have enough. They decide to sell Joseph into slavery, telling their father Jacob that he was torn apart by wild beasts. Jacob goes into deep mourning, but the young Joseph, after many adventures and some strategic dreams ends up the most powerful man in Egypt, holding the keys to its abundant granaries at a time of worldwide famine."

Rob's voice streams from the screen ahead of me. "Jacob," he continues, "also known as Israel, and his clan are starving back in Canaan—the Promised Land—so he sends his sons down to Egypt to procure supplies. They appear as supplicants before Joseph, whom they do not recognize even though he recognizes them. Joseph puts the brothers through many tests in which they reveal that they have grown in compassion, just as he has grown in humility. Joseph finally reveals himself to his brothers and forgives them for selling him into slavery, since it now seems plain that God, who appears for the first time in this whole story, had sent him ahead to insure the survival of Jacob's clan, the seventy nomads who at this point comprise the whole people of Israel. The brothers speed back to Canaan to tell the tidings to their father Jacob, and to prepare to bring their starving family back to Egypt under Joseph's protection."

I look up to see my brother's video image standing behind the podium. He is wearing glasses that, because of the extreme thinness of his face, appear very large. He is wearing a dark indigo suit, elegant in its tailoring, and a fine white shirt, and a richly colored tie. I try to look at his clothes and not the painful unevenness of his skin, the roughened red sores and fleshy welts of the Kaposi's sarcoma I'd forgotten about. As I'd forgotten the beard that can only barely cover the sores. And forgotten, too, the sharpened jut of his cheekbones and that of his chin, and the thinning high arch of his nose. Such physical details really do melt away in memory, just as my friends who earlier had lost people they loved to illness told me they would. Rob turns directly to the camera and pauses. He smiles, long in the tooth. And says: "The lines upon which I'd like to focus begin when Jacob interrupts the brothers' telling of their news. Here is my own translation.

"'I don't need to hear anymore,' said Israel. 'If my son Joseph is still alive then I will go and see him before I die.' So Israel set out with all he had and he came to Beersheba and offered up sacrifices to the God of his father Isaac. And God called out to Israel in a vision by night, 'Jacob, Jacob.' And Jacob answered, 'Here I am.' And the vision said, 'I am the Lord, the God of your fathers. Do not fear to go down into Egypt, for I will make you a great nation there. I will go down with you to Egypt, and I myself will also bring you back up, and Joseph's hand shall close your eyes.'"

Rob turns his head as does any good speaker. He is taking his audience into his gaze: those on the left, those on the right, those sitting or standing in the back. Many of these the camera does not attempt to record; they are simply assumed to be present. Rob is looking out toward them with his deep, dark eyes, liquid with their full shine and shadow.

He says slowly, "Think of the worlds these five lines contain. First you have Jacob, who after a lifetime of loss is now weary, wary, passive, and self-pitying. And still he is also Israel, the man of wholeness who earned his name by wrestling all night with an Angel of God, and who now, once more, slashes through to the essential. He doesn't care about the details, or even the consequences; all he knows is that before he dies, he must see his son Joseph. There is a clarity of purpose that comes when one acknowledges the closeness of death. Jacob in one stroke declares that he will leave the land which God has promised to his grandfather Abraham and go down into

Egypt — the country his father Isaac had been expressly forbidden to visit. Jacob is alone, out on a limb — like Lear, he is a great ruined tower of a man out in the darkness. But where Lear looks into the void, learns compassion, and goes mad," Rob says, "Jacob is vouchsafed a vision: A voice calls tenderly out of the darkness, acknowledges him, and takes his hand. The voice of God speaks of the descent that is necessary for the ascent, the exile that is necessary for the return, the turning away from the Promised Land that is necessary for the promise to be fulfilled. The vision is challenging, expansive: God will make Israel a great nation — the small band of nomads will become the six hundred thousand souls who will later stand at Sinai. But it is also loving and tender, as small as the promise that Jacob will die in his beloved son Joseph's arms, that Joseph's hand will gently close his eyes for the final time."

The camera dips. My brother has been moved slightly from the center of the focus. His left shoulder and arm are out of the frame. Then the lens zooms in and finds his face just as he lowers his head. He clears his throat, seems to be glancing down at what must be a page of his own transcript under the bar of the frame. His jaw tightens. When he looks up, he has a slightly somber smile. The glasses hide his eyes. "But for me," he continues, his voice rough, "the whole miracle of these lines is contained in two of its simplest words: Jacob's *'Heneini'* — 'Here I am'—and God's *'A-raid'* — 'I will go down.' God calls Jacob's name twice — once, perhaps, to wake him, and the second time to call him totally to himself. And through all his conflicts and confusion Jacob is able to answer, 'Here I am.' He knows who he is and where he stands, and he is able to clear his heart and open himself fully to God's words.

"How I envy," Rob says, "our forefathers and mothers who could hear the voice of God with such utter directness. God tells Jacob, the man of so many wanderings, that he has to make one more journey. But this is not to be like most human journeys — a stumbling in the dark — for God parts the veil for one moment, giving Jacob a vision of the Exodus which is still four hundred years away. And most important of all, God says *'A-raid'* — 'I will go down' — promising not only that He will watch over the people of Israel in their exile, sending blessings from above, but that He shares the exile with us. He walks right by our sides.

"The name for 'Egypt' in Hebrew, *'Mitzrayim,'* is rooted in the Hebrew words for narrow, constricted, and also for sorrow. For Jacob and the people of Israel, Egypt is the promise of food in a starving time; it is a haven, even if it will soon become a narrow place, a land of bondage. What God's words in this passage teach us is that we must honor Israel's descent into Egypt as reverently as we celebrate our deliverance from it. The narrow place is a source of sorrow, but it can also be a birth canal." Someone moans, and the camera, as if startled, pans across front rows, pulled toward the source of the abrupt cry. There is a shuffling, a shifting of weight, but as the camera's lens scans across the rows the congregation seems a single mass, no one turning about or standing out. Robert says, "The important thing to remember, even when we descend into a place of constriction and pain, is that God goes with us.

"In my own spiritual path," he says, then pauses, "I have had to descend into a narrow place. My world for the last ten years has been scourged and straitened by AIDS. It is a world where, unlike God's promise to Jacob, the sons do not close their fathers' eyes, but fathers close their sons'. Almost all the friends I thought I would be growing old with are already dead or dying. My own body each day contrives a new betrayal. For someone who once leapt onto airplanes to cover a revolution in Iran or a CIA bungle in Cambodia, the seven-block walk from my house to the ocean now seems as much as I can handle. The world is getting smaller, tighter, lonelier. Yet even in this Egypt of AIDS I am full of gratitude for the havens I have found, uplifted and transformed when I have felt the nearness of God. When I see how lovers kiss away each other's sores; when I see a father massage his son's swollen feet, help him to the toilet, brush his teeth; when I see friends, hideously young, face their deaths with bravery and grace, I know that God has accompanied us into our exile, into our very narrow place.

"God cannot save us from suffering, but He can accompany us, and in the moments of our true wholeness, we can feel his love. God does not spare us our sorrows, but sometimes He makes us worthy of them. God stood by Israel in our Egyptian exile even though it took us four hundred years to finally call out to Him and to devise a path for our own deliverance.

"We make our journeys in the dark. God is with us but we so rarely feel His presence. What my studies with my miraculous teachers, what my ever-deeper life of meditation and prayer has taught me, is the sustaining power of a spiritual discipline.

"When we were finally ready to return from Egypt to the Promised Land, God did not whisk us there on a magic carpet. We had to put one foot before the other. We had to wander and squabble, feeling hunger and despair, and even when we arrived we were not sure where we were or what to do. The Jewish path is tough; instead of answers, we are given *mitzvot*, good deeds and duties, ways to bring holiness into our lives by action and discipline. In our tradition, the reward for fulfilling one *mitzvah* is the opportunity to perform another. Still, for me, this is a path of meaning, a path of sustaining joy."

I glance up, a final glance, knowing how my eyes can get in the way of my hearing.

The tape looks to be moving quickly now, though the speed has not increased. Static is breaking through the illusion and veracity of the image. In the center of the lens stands a haggard, gaunt, and gleaming man. He looks out, his face scoured and marked. His gaze is incomprehensibly gentle.

"I have no idea," he continues, his voice thin and wind-lost, but persisting, "what the ultimate purpose of my own particular descent into the narrow place of AIDS might be. I am even willing to believe that, in itself, it has no purpose at all. What I do know, however, is that the work of our lives is the making of our meaning, so that we may ultimately link up with the source of all meaning, the *Ein Sof*, blessed be He. We bless each other and we bless God when we do our work wholeheartedly — knowing what is important, fulfilling our duties, our *mitzvot*, and acting in the world in as righteous and as loving a way as possible.

"In deepest humility," Robert says, to finish, "I take on this holy charge to be a *maggid*, a teacher in the community of Israel. I can only promise that I will work faithfully for as long as I am given. And I can only pray that when God calls out my name, I can answer with some of the heartfelt clarity of Jacob, *Heneini*. Here I am."

Static streams across the screen.

I do not press stop when his face disappears.

Exhalations

There is a point beyond which our senses cannot lead us.
— DIANE ACKERMAN

A death is like a symphony. It holds that much energy and that much concerted work. Whether life leaves a body quickly or slowly, every cell plays its part. The coordination is intricate and tremendous. No noise. Much noise. Stillness. Thrashing. The full outtake of breath.

Voice is vibration. Life is vibration. Our lives begin with a cry, an exhalation, and an exhalation is how we go out.

Sometimes the people we love surround us at the end. They hear us stop.

I have stories to tell about the long hours when my brother turned his face from us to move through his death, and I have a strong aversion to making the final shape singular and smooth. I do not want the parts to cease vibrating. I do not want them to cohere as if one. I'd rather let the parts be what they are — parts, not the body whole. I prefer to let them be alive in themselves. That is how they seem to me. Alive, meaning: unfinished. Alive, meaning: energy moving.

The family was scattered all over the country.

Let me distance myself from where I've been headed and pause for a second to posit a situation. All right. You ready?

Your brother is dying far away from you. No one has called and said so, but you know it. How do you know it? Simply, you do. Have you felt the loose float of a thread from a spider strike your face as you walk? It is something like that, but not. More than a disturbance in the air, it is something ex- and internal that tugs. It is a message of a sort, though it has neither printed words nor words formed through sound. And if, as is the usual reflex, you erase the message, or the feeling, or the thought, in the same half-instant that it comes to you, then later on — perhaps days or years later — you will work hard to bring to consciousness even the smallest fragment. What were you doing then — which moment? What made you know: here was a message. You'll ask yourself these questions; you know that you will. And maybe you will reclaim the sequence and maybe you will have to bind up the vacancy with cocoon silk, wish, and speculation. Maybe it was . . . , you'll say, going back over things. With every good intention you might put forward a sensible fiction of what, when, and how. But you will want something to hold for yourself. There was a moment when such difficult information came to you. You will want to go on and tell others about it, how you learned part of your life was gone. The part of full life that was his. He was gone from his life, and yours.

Maybe my parents phoned and in some oblique way told me. Maybe I knew from keeping in constant contact with Rob's household. Nothing was spelled out, but everything was understood. No one used the word *decision*. Physically, I was at a distance; I was supposed to remain where I was. Robert had made my role clear, without having to say so aloud. Support from a distance. Sounding board. Confidante. Certainly he had completed his research, thought through the sequence of possible scenes, positioned the players, but had not yet snapped the board and called: "Action!"

I understood that he could not have me at his bedside. Not

three weeks before, I'd visited him in California. It was dead winter in New England, late February, and Santa Monica with its flowering hills, palm trees, and outdoor cafés was a postcard come to life. As much as I enjoyed the ease and beauty of the landscape, I didn't trust it. I didn't believe it had bedrock. A perfection built atop fissures just feels too careful. Almost always, Rebecca and I visited Robert and Gary together, but this time she flew back home after a few days and I stayed longer with them on my own. I spent that week trying to be of use — grocery shopping, cooking meals, twisting strong-stemmed lemons off the backyard trees to hand-squeeze for pitchers of fresh lemonade, driving Robert to medical appointments and Metivta discussion groups and to Ohr Ha Torah Sabbath services. At the same time, I was just a sister, happy to be present to take up once again the old habit of hanging about.

On my last Santa Monica afternoon, Rob called to me from his bedroom. I'd been sitting in the living room, talking with Tom, his college friend who was visiting for the weekend, and Carol, who had flown in for a few days from New York City, and Gary, who although glad for the company and help, also craved a return to his and Rob's privacy and peace. We four were just chatting. When I heard Robert call my name, I got up from the immense overstuffed couch and made my way down the spine of the dim hall.

The bedroom was very Californian — light tones, soft textures, sunlight at the windows. Rob was propped up against the pillows, the top sheet sprawled across him, the blanket thrown off and tangled on the other half of the bed. As a child, he used to kick his covers into tight twists at the foot of his bed. I'd walk past his open door in the morning and see the upheaval. It used to amaze me that he had this secret active life at night; I slept in place — covers lying as smoothly ordered as they'd been when I'd pulled them about me the night before. Now as I crossed past the semi-antiqued wooden desk he'd brought with him from New York, the tumult of his blankets seemed earned; they looked like a Sanskrit word for the fight for sleep. I heard the battle waged throughout the night in Rob's hacking coughs and strangled gasping for breath. That's got to be it, he's cleared his lungs now, or this, this one has got to be the last. I'd wake in a start, holding my breath, as if my denial might help him breathe cleanly.

"Hey, Rob-chu," I said, our grandmother's endearment for him. I sat down at the bottom edge of the huge bed, atop the blanket, but not directly on the sheets, which were stained here and there in small brown blotches of old blood. This wouldn't be blood he'd coughed up. This would be from the sores. And now accepted as if a design pattern of tiny buds. And many times washed, but no longer as optimistically or laboriously bleached. And you can't catch AIDS, can't get infected, by sitting near the shadows of blood.

From the edge of his bed, I said, "How was your nap?"

He smiled his wryly diffident smile — that old superiority? — and lightly answered, "Oh, just fine." One eye was covered by a gauze pad and bandaged. The other eye, deep brown, was fixed on me. "I figured that this would be a good time to talk," he said. "Tomorrow you're leaving."

"I've got the taxi reserved for the airport. I set it up with the dispatcher already, just how you told me, so there's no foul-up. The cab's coming to pick me up at 8:15. My flight is at 9:50. Are you positive that's early enough for me to make it, given the morning rush hour? It was a huge mess getting out here."

"You'll make it with time to spare."

"I hate flying."

"Oh, it's nothing. More accidents happen on the ground than in the air, Marcie. I flew all the time, everywhere."

I sighed heavily. Looking at him, I said directly, "I hate going. I don't want to leave you."

"No," he said. "You have to go back. Rebecca's waiting for you."

A good conversation discovers its own heart slowly, by listening to the rhythm of word and silence, by feeling the beating effort and desire at the center of the words. So it was for us then, that afternoon. Rob sat back against the soft full pillows. I edged closer to him with each sentence. Between us were the small rills of the mattress and the sheet stretched atop them with its map, the tracings of the illness that kept shaking and wounding him, the fluids that, still flowing, sustained him. "Are you afraid?" I asked finally.

He told me he wasn't. He said that he truly was not.

"I'm afraid," I said.

"I know you are," he said. "I wish you weren't."

"What do you think is going to — do you think we go on after this? I don't mean heaven, I guess, but some kind of consciousness or energy? Some other way of being?"

Slowly, he shook his head. "I don't know."

I felt the breath go out of me. "You don't."

Again he shook his head. His beautiful strong face was gaunt, and I know that his skin was broken by lesions, but now, conjuring the past, I can no longer see the illness on him. I really cannot, although I understand as if by checklist how he looked then. I recall the bandage and gauze mounded above one eye. I recall the beard, grown when he could no longer accept the scrape of a razor.

Rob said, "I don't know if there's anything more. But I'm not sure if that's the point, my knowing what's next. I've thought about it, and I really believe that I've done what I set out to do with my life. Only thing is, I didn't expect to have to do it all quite this quickly." He leaned his head against the wall and gave a short, self-deprecatory laugh. "I'm not afraid of what's coming my way. You know, don't you, that there is, there has always been, something coming next?"

"Robert, just wait. Stop, okay?"

He gazed at me.

"I love our conversations," I blurted out. Then in the next moment we were holding each other. I was sobbing against the shoulder of his T-shirt, my mouth open for air against the thin cloth, which, like the bedsheet, was stained. "I'm going to miss you. Robert, I'm going to miss you."

"I'm going to miss you, too," he said. He was squeezing me hard.

I held on to him. He held me.

That was our real good-bye.

"What happened?"

Three friends looked up from various large pieces of furniture as I reentered the living room. I'm sure my face was red and eyes swimming, but inside one word balanced me: solace.

"We talked," I said. I sat down, taking a place among them again. They looked away quickly, as if no more of any honesty could be said. I repeated, my voice quiet as thought, "We talked."

> Everything is as it should be, nothing will
> ever change, nobody will ever die.
> — VLADIMIR NABOKOV

Again: on the day Robert made his decision maybe our parents, who were visiting him, telephoned and in some oblique way told me what they thought might come next, or maybe I was informed by keeping in constant contact with Rob's household.

However, I don't think either is the case. I believe that I simply sensed the truth. The words that would have mattered never got spoken aloud. Still, there are disturbances and low rumblings that we take in across distance with our whole bodies. Low in the throat, deep in the heart, we are speaking and listening. We keep feeling what we can't hear.

The house in Santa Monica was filled with comings and goings. There besides Mom and Dad were Cliff, Marie, and their young son, Jake. Clifford, the sibling who as a child possessed the annoying mischievousness of a long-legged, laughing, energy-mad imp, who was the team captain and varsity athlete that Robert was not, had years before grown into a sturdy-souled man. He and "the baby," Dan, who also had grown up, though in his own almost sorely tender way, had remained in Cleveland to raise families. Now Cliff, and Marie, and nine-year-old Jacob were staying in the house in Santa Monica. (Anneli, five years old and born shortly after our grandmother Anna's death in 1989, was back in Cleveland; Dan and Paula were taking care of her, along with their children, four-year-old Jordan and five-week-old infant Haley.)

I was in Boston. Rebecca was away for meetings in Washington, D.C. It was March across the entire continent, though the same month made for different conditions across the many miles.

Maybe my parents telephoned.

The family was scattered across the country.

It is in the way of certain stories to tell themselves to each other, and so it happens here that an older story speaks up. My great-aunt Ethel told me this while we were riding in the long black car following her dear sister's — and my grandmother's — casket. Robert was in the limousine, and Cliff and Dan, and Mom and Dad. As Nonny's only remaining sister, the one she had been able to get out of Europe and bring to America, saving her from the Nazis' vile certainties, Aunt Ethel was a passenger in the dark-windowed limo, as well. To my comment that Nonny had in effect "decided" her death, that with what faculties Alzheimer's had left her, she'd made the decision no longer to eat, Aunt Ethel said, "Our grandmother decided her death, too."

"Our grandmother? You're saying — ? Wait, who are you talking about?"

Aunt Ethel smiled wistfully. "Ach, how could you know?" Her face was small and bright-eyed — hazel eyes, as her sister's had been — the skin soft and wrinkled, wreathed many times over. "I meant my grandmother, and your Nonny's grandmother. Terese Dagenstein."

The limo was braking. Outside the tinted windows, the snow was plowed up against the curbs in high mounds, as if the trenches of the Great War lay hidden on the other side of all that white. The black branches of the oaks and maples were bowed by ice; some limbs were splintered and cracked, the yellowish fibers of wood glittering with crystals. It was a midwestern February and far below zero; everything frozen. The ground would not take in a casket to the regulation depth because the earth even above the frost line was unyielding. Nonny's casket would have to rest in a too-shallow grave during the service and, handful by handful, get only lightly covered. Afterward, the big shovels would go back to work, deepening the hold. Before dark — we'd been promised — others hands would lower her casket and fill up the space.

"What do you mean she decided, Aunt Ethel?"

"Well," she said, gently and not unhappily, leaning closer to speak, "our grandmother was old. And she felt she had lived long. She was very tired. She could no longer see well. One day she looked over and asked, 'Who is in the room with me?' And I said, 'I am here — Etel's here.' She liked me. She said, 'Etel, I am going to turn my face to the wall and I will fall to sleep. It will be a very deep sleep. In the morning, when Mother comes in' — she meant, my mother, her own daughter, this was back in Szacsur — 'in the morning, when Mother comes in,' she said, 'tell her not to wake me. For if she does, it would be a very great sin.'" Aunt Ethel sat back against the high seat of the passenger compartment. We were all listening. Her eyelids fluttered briefly, and she nodded, as if seeing again an old woman, a dear person, the shape of her back on a bed. "She put her head down on the pillow. And after a few days," she said, "with her face turned to the wall, she died."

"She decided," I whispered. A small thrill went through me; a small surge of strength.

"Yes," my great-aunt said, as the limousine, second in line, smoothly carried the seven of us forward, "she died."

"We had no idea how much he'd been suffering. His nose wouldn't stop bleeding. He bled from his eyes," my sister-in-law Marie said, her voice low and urgent. "The sinuses were pressing against the bones and cartilage and they were about to give way. On Thursday night, he made a decision. I remember we were sitting around the table in their dining area. We'd finished dessert some time before. I'd already put Jake to bed back in the back guest bedroom. Your parents were there, and Cliff and I, and Gary. Robert said something and everyone looked at him. He was talking out loud, but more as if he was just figuring things out as he went along. Nothing was firm. I remember someone said, 'Well, who would you want? Who would you ask to be there?'"

Cliff cut in then, his hands clasped in front of him, between his knees. He said, "Robert looked around the table. He didn't say Marie's name. He just pointed and said" — suddenly Cliff pointed and swung around to his wife — "'Her.'"

Marie sat bolt upright to my left on the couch in their home outside of Cleveland. This was during our most recent conversation. We've gone over the story, time and again, nearly every other time I come for a visit from Boston. Something in it will not rest. Now, Marie's face was red with the effort of calling up the details. Her eyes, direct and blue, were flashing as if the irises were responding to something immense and bright coming round the corner right at her. She is a woman of quiet strength and generous consolation; that Rob asked her to be with him is a fact that I've never questioned.

"The next morning," Cliff said, falling back in the rocker, the chair pitching back with his weight, "we woke up" — he nodded at Marie — "and just sort of looked at each other like, is this really going to happen?"

"I'm confused," I said. "When did you see the — you know. You know what I mean."

Cliff let out a breath, half-laugh, half-grief. "Yeah, right. I almost forgot again. Well. Well, it was on the night he decided, Thursday — after I got up from the table. Everyone was wandering about. I heard a little boy crying. I went into the living room, because I had an image of a little boy huddled in a corner. No one there. I opened the slats of the shutters to look out to the front yard. No one. But the crying — ! I turned back to the hall just to see where I'd been, and there it was. Crossing the hall at an angle, there it — it was heading into Rob's room." He looked down at his clenched fists.

I prodded him. "What did it look like?"

Reluctantly he said, "Reddish brown hair. Beautiful skin, very pale."

"Male or female?"

"It wasn't about that kind of — oh, I guess a female."

"Wings?"

"Wings, or whatever, at the shoulders, flat." He looked up,

almost angrily. "I wasn't concentrating on those things! What you're asking now didn't matter to me. It clearly was from another dimension. Everything about it was intense and remote. I knew that I couldn't yell, 'Hey, you!' There was no use in my speaking. I wasn't the reason. It moved with a purpose. It wasn't looking for me. The hallway isn't wide — two strides across — I don't know how long it took reaching Rob's door, it could have lasted ten lifetimes.

"I took one step toward the threshold and sort of stumbled. It was clearly there for Robert, and yet I was seeing it, so somehow it was there for me, too. I wasn't happy. I was — I felt, why me? I couldn't understand, I couldn't make earthly sense of it. I was upset. The angel was in Robert's room by then."

"And the little boy?"

"Still crying," he said quietly, the chair rocking him forward. "I heard him. I think it was Rob's soul that was crying."

Cliff said that he went back into the kitchen, where Marie was rinsing the meal's glasses and plates at the sink. Clink by clink the pieces of china were carefully placed into the dishwasher's opened racks. "I stood next to her and I kind of mumbled, 'Marie, death is in the house.' Then I told her what happened. She said that she already knew."

"I told him," she said softly, turning to me, "that I didn't see what he saw, but I'd felt the direction in the house, the movement. I felt the force of it."

"Then," Cliff continued, "we tried to be normal. We tried to dismiss it. I remember later, we all went into the bedroom. We were hanging out on their bed and watching *Jeopardy* on TV. Robert beat everyone. He always knew the questions to the answers. Then he just said, 'I've decided. I'm sure. Tomorrow's the day.' The next morning, Marie and I woke up, that's when we looked at each other, and wondered what was real." He steadied the rocker and let his body stay still.

I paused. "Dad thinks that what you heard and saw that night were hallucinations. He says you were under a lot of stress. Hallucinations can be auditory, too; they're not only visual. He says it's understandable."

Cliff said, "No."

I might have telephoned that night from Boston, or someone staying with Rob — maybe our parents — might have phoned me. I believe that it was not that Thursday evening but in the couple of days before, when Rob was so weak and ravaged that he lay in a haze of sleep and pain, when I placed the call into what I believed was a vigil. I was in my study. The connection to the coast went through with a series of clicks, then the receiver was picked up in the house in Santa Monica, quickly, by the second ring. "Hello?" someone said

"Hi, this is Rob's sister. How is he, how's he doing?"

"Marcie!"

"What?"

"This is Rob."

"No! But you sound too young."

"I do?"

"Yes," I said, gripping the phone, "your voice sounds young. You sound like a boy again. I haven't heard you like this in years. I didn't think I'd get a chance to speak again — " I tried to steady my emotions, so they wouldn't get in the way. "How are you?"

"I wasn't good." More quietly he said, "I was in a coma. I woke up a while ago. Then when I saw where I was, I was disappointed. Marcie, I was disappointed to be here. Back with everyone, again."

"Oh," I said, and it came out as a groan.

"I'm so tired. I need to move on."

I put into my voice as much balm and peace as I could muster. "It's not time."

"The back and forth is getting much harder."

"This conversation is our bonus, okay? Robert, I love you."

"Yes. I love you, too." And a few moments later, he set down the phone.

"I didn't think he would do it," Mom said slowly, her voice grainy and thick with sadness. "You know why? Because Friday brings Sabbath. I thought to myself, he's religious and he won't want to risk disturbing the day of rest."

It was beautiful that Friday morning in March. In Santa Monica it was spring, and the blossoms were fragrant, the sun was shining. Cliff and Marie woke in the guest room and looked at each other, wondering what was real. Their son, Jacob, was asleep in the alcove. They woke him, and went into the main part of the house. Mom and Dad were there. Then Robert and Gary came out of the master bedroom. Robert walked on his own, effortlessly, as if again healthy. He moved freely. They all commented on it, how happy he looked without plastic IV tubes attached and hanging from him. The shunts that had jutted out of his wrists and chest for the drip-in medications also were gone. There would be no more medicine to battle the disease, only to hasten and ease his way out of pain. Whatever anyone knew or suspected about what might come to him next, everyone later told me the same thing: Robert was shining. He was wearing the peach silk pajamas Ron had given him years before, a gift of sensory indulgence, beauty, and love. Gary, whose love was making its final gift, was at his side now, wan and worried, his lean face tight, mouth grim, but moving steadily forward, nonetheless.

Mom went up to Robert and took his hands. "His eyes," she

later told me, "were full of light. I couldn't stop looking at them. I'd never seen them like that before. And his hands, he had such beautiful hands. I just couldn't imagine what — I just couldn't. I could only say stupid things, I hate it that I didn't tell him all that I felt, I could only say silly, stupid things. I told him his hands were beautiful. And his eyes, I told him about his eyes." She looked away from me. "It wasn't right."

Robert had just said to her, "Mom, I want you to take Dad home." He turned next to Dad, and said, "I know you don't believe in the God of your father, but I hope one day you will accept the God of your son." He hugged them both and told them they had been good parents, and then he said, looking from one to the other: "I'm eager for my next adventure."

Everyone was propelled by Robert's decision. There was nothing more to think about, just things to do. Something larger than individual desire was taking over. Everyone was in motion. Robert, frail as he was, stood poised at the center. When Jake crossed the room to hug his uncle, Robert opened his arms and leaned back. Suddenly he was lifting the nine-year-old up over his head. Rob looked up into Jacob's giggling face and said, "Oh, I used to do this to you all the time when you were a little baby." Locking eyes, the boy and the man laughed. Robert used his last physical strength for that. When he set Jacob down, everyone kept moving out from the center.

> Power resides in the moment of transition
> from a past to a new state.
> — EMERSON

"Your mom kept muttering, 'This isn't right, this isn't right,'" Marie told me. "She was packing their bags and she had this kind of bulldog expression. She didn't want to leave him, but he was making them go. He couldn't have them there, if he was going to keep going. He couldn't have the immediate family with him. He needed to let go, and wasn't sure he would be able to if the family was near. I don't know how she did it. I don't know that I could have done what your parents did. Your dad was quiet; it was so tough for him. He kissed Robert good-bye at the door, and tried his best to keep walking.

"When everyone left, Rob just collapsed. I rocked him. It wasn't verbal language, I just held him like a baby. His posture wasn't scared, or fetal; but the sense of it was that now he could go on, and he'd made his peace with the world. I said to him, 'I feel like you're going to be okay.' And he said, 'I know, Marie. I will be.' Then his nose started to bleed. It was a very dramatic shift from the person who was glowing and could say good-bye, to someone bleeding out."

Mom said, "I grabbed Nonny's three-branched silver candelabra from their mantel, the matching half of the pair, you know, to the one you have. I needed it. I think I said something to Gary, like, 'Don't send the *gendarmes* after me.' Of all things! I was thinking about *Les Miserables,* how Jean Valjean stole from the priest so he could make his way from prison — they'd given him nothing — and how the priest knew he'd been robbed, but because he knew why, he didn't want to report the theft. Well," she said, and her head dropped, "we flew home. On the plane, and then in the car, I kept it with me. I just held on to it. I still have it."

Dad said, "We came into the house around five or six o'clock at night, some six hours later, and phoned California. Robert was sleeping, they said. We thought, well, maybe he's going to be fine. You know, people pull out of things. They change their minds. Our minds are so powerful, no one knows how much they affect. I wanted Robert to keep fighting and beat that disease. That's what I wanted."

Mom glanced at him sharply. "Gene," she said.

"Ah, heck." Dad shook his head with a sigh. "We put down the phone, and then I picked it back up. That's when we phoned you, just to say how things were." With a curt laugh, he said, "As if we knew. But we had to talk to you. And we had to phone Danny to check on them and the kids. He and Paula had the babies. I wanted to speak to the children before they went to bed. I wanted to be able to tell them good night."

I don't believe my parents' call was the first. I am certain I understood before sundown — perhaps as early as that morning — what was happening, but now when I think back, I recall only the agitation of Friday night. When Rebecca phoned in from Washington, D.C., in the evening, I was wandering around the house as if there were some hidden door inside that I should find.

"Bec, I don't know what I can do," I said raggedly into the mouthpiece. "I can't keep calling there. The last time I did was two hours ago, and Gary answered and said no one could stop to talk with me. Rob was in a coma, but it wasn't peaceful, it was work."

"You have to wait." Her voice was deliberate and calm. "That's what you have to do." She paused, then rushed ahead: "I'm so sorry. I'm sorry. I tried to get a flight out, but they're stopped, it's too late. I wish I could be with you."

"I know."

"Or do you want to go over to someone's house? You can call a friend, go over there — anyone would tell you to come over."

"No, no, I'm waiting here. This is my home."

The night howled. Down the street, the branches cut across each other in the wind and every window in the house was battling and shaking. I wandered back to the kitchen. Although I'd only lit Sabbath candles every now and then over the years, I took down my grandmother's candleholders, the small ones, not the candelabra, and put in two white new candles. I flicked off the overhead. In darkness, I lit the wicks. The dual flames shot up, wax sputtering, and held. I waved the real glow toward me three times and said the blessing to welcome the day of rest. *Baruch atah Adonai. . . . Blessed are You, Adonai, our God. . . .*

Silent, I dropped my arms. A little uncertainly I added in a whisper: "Please welcome my brother, Robert." More forcefully I repeated it. Then I said it again, even louder. I wanted to hear what it was I was asking. And I wanted the entreaty to move outward.

I wandered into the living room, uncertain what else to do but wait for word.

Who can put the narrative of the ending together? Who edits out one action or moment, and highlights another? Shall I go breath by breath and speak of the stories others have told me, saving their moments of his death from oblivion? Shall I speak of Robert lying in bed, his two rabbis singing to him after the three of them had read from the Psalms, and Rob's rabbi, who in the course of their studies had also become his friend, saying of Robert (so I've been told), "Never have I heard anyone read so beautifully," or many hours later, leaning toward him to whisper in parting, "Good night, sweet prince, and flights of angels sing you to your rest." Shall I let Cliff speak of being sent from the house with his young son and, at a loss what to do, yielding to the child's pleas that they take a tour of a movie studio, so that the hours his own brother spent dying, he was a

93

witness to one smirky make-believe set after another? Or shall I speak in summary of Marie and Gary, tending to Rob? Rob coming out of his coma to make peace with Gary by saying, "Are you going to be okay?" and not closing his eyes until he heard an answer. Of the weather turning? Torrents of rain and dark wind flailing the stucco-walled house? Of Rob, hearing the news as he struggled, that his friend had just given birth to a boy and that its middle name would honor his, and saying: "Isn't the world wonderful? One life is entering as another departs." Of the two hours of stillness beginning there around two A.M. where Marie looked into his face as he lay unconscious, and wondered what work he was completing as he breathed into his death? Of my lifting my head from my pillow in Boston and saying clearly, as if responding to someone else in a conversation, though I'd been sleeping: "I'm grateful." And hearing my words, I look in surprise at the clock: 5:23. Of Rebecca in a hotel room in Washington, D.C., packing to fly home, noticing the hands on her bright new watch had stopped cold at 5:25. Of the final waves that ripped through Robert just before dawn? Or of the blood on his teeth and dryness of his face, the agonized expression his features wore as his emptied body was zipped into the corded bag? How he'd found the current, and on it the slow open boat?

Not mine to save. Not mine. Let all this go. Their stories. His story. Mine. Exhalations. Exhalations.

Afterwords

There are voices and calls that sound out loud,
yet one fails to hear them, and there are others
that make no sound at all, yet they are heard.
— RABBI ADOLF (ABRAHAM) ALTMANN

And was that the end? Was Rob's death the end?

Here is what I always come back to: a close-up of my hands clearing away shrunken, winter-battered leaves. I am bending down to the soil, which is beginning to darken with moisture, but really the season ahead is still a bare promise. Spring is just a tendency the earth tilts toward. I am not thinking much of anything. Kneeling beneath the huge maple next to the house, I am fully absorbed. At the most, a few weeds might poke through the shade blanketing this strip of dirt when warmth hits, but I scratch around the knobby roots anyway, dislodging frayed, grayish helicopter seeds, gravelly stones, dank masses of leaf debris. More housekeeper than gardener, I clear off the surface. It is early morning, the street quiet: only my hands, leaves, seeds stirring. A life of small actions. Shuss, shuss, shuss.

Then, inside the same moment that my hands sift the soil, everything is different. Sound has pulled away. The outside of the world stops. Without a blink of the eyes I am looking into another kind of space. In my head, fully formed, are a half-dozen words that are not mine. The words are all in one box, one bar, right? You know how a message is put together, both abbreviated and whole, on telegrams in those old movies?

These six words are like that — suddenly just *there,* complete as one unit, not thought out word by word. The communication says in a voice other than human, a chime without tones: *Robert inducted into a higher order.*

I rock back on my heels. I don't utter a sound. I can't pretend not to know. The message feels *placed.* It is placed somehow at the very center of my brain and yet — I know this sounds odd — also in front, blocking out thoughts of my own. I don't know quite what I mean by drawing these coordinates, except that there was a sense of proximity and materiality, and I need to be as honest as I can. That message was separate in my mind, as if I could see it and hear it, although of course in terms of the physical senses neither was true. It was like being confronted by the real mystery in a voice, which is not the passage and transmission of its sound, but of its intelligence. Sound may be only one way a voice calls our attention. Here was a voice so shot through with its message, so translucent with meaning, meaning was all that it was. Intelligence in one clear soundless note.

I went absolutely hollow as if I were an automaton. I didn't stop to let myself feel or think, or I knew I'd find a way to erase what had been sent. People push away gifts all the time that they can't explain. Quickly I walked to the front yard and up the four steps of the house. I went upstairs to my study and found my desk calendar, each week marked at its start by a splendidly photographed nature scene. I flipped the glossy pages to the date. The blank one-inch-by-five-inch slot was tagged in its lower right corner by the publisher with a quasi-holiday detail: *Earth Day.* In the tiniest letters I've ever inked, I recorded the words of the message exactly as they were given. I used just a small triangle of the whole rectangle, because I was embarrassed by what I was doing. April 22, 1995: *Robert inducted into a higher order.* It seemed so odd, what it said, that I was writing it down, that the marks I made were miniature. But if I didn't write it down I knew I'd allow myself easy as pie to forget it. You know what I'm trying to say? In some deep part of myself, there would always be a bruise, that I'd let it happen. That I'd let this gift go. I'd let myself forget.

So I wrote the words. Then under them, again in nearly infinitesimal print, but in all capital letters so that it would stand apart as my comment, I penned one other word: HAPPINESS.

Isn't it strange that a person can feel embarrassed and happy about the same sentence?

The thing is, receiving that message did not stop me from grieving. You'd think that it would have, but I still had to go through my own life. I'd lost my brother and the ways I missed him were numerous and complicated. Despite the comforts of a loving relationship and the number of good friends surrounding me, I felt depressed and lonely and at ends. Oh, I believed what I'd been told about Rob that April morning — I still do. As I said, those words weren't mine. But outside of a very small circle, I don't share what happened. In fact, whenever I have thought to do so, I can't remember the verb that puts the whole message in motion. Sometimes I go find the calendar stored in a back cupboard to look it up. *Inducted* — a formal word, or militaristic. Robert was *inducted*. And: *into a higher order.* Is this of energies, or spirits, or intelligences? Just as I don't rush to speak about the experience, I don't keep trying to analyze its meaning. Also, what I haven't mentioned aloud to anybody: I recall something else. I recall, as if behind the words, the glimmering movement of a faint presence. Only the merest sense of an image: the shimmer of a long pale table, beyond it perhaps a podium, and one tier above, also with a stately aspect, a taller structure. Three tiers: a tribunal of sorts. The worded message was foremost, but the space from which the words might have been issued was offered up too — palimpsest.

The voice wasn't my brother's, nor any individual's. It was a voice of community. If Robert did play a part in informing me, he participated as would the designee of any honor: he would have proffered the names of those to be notified, in celebration, in pride, in relief, in farewell. On a new stage, perhaps, Rob was producing again — doing the research, writing the words, selecting the site, positioning everybody just so. (Let's have Marcie bending near the maple tree, fingers in dirt. Here she goes. Very good. Sound! Action! Let's roll it.)

How could I presume to pin down anything about this experience, except that it happened? As Robert said, now long ago, as he lay in his sickbed and I asked if he believed in something waiting for us after death: "I'm not sure that's the point, my knowing what comes next. I've thought about it, and I really think I've done what I've set out to do in my life. . . . You know, don't you, that there is, there has always been, something coming next."

In any case, living — inducted? — on this plane, and not any other, I can hardly ever hold on to the whole short message as it was given to me under the maple tree. But then, my brother Cliff has the same relationship with the angel he saw moving swiftly past on the night before Robert died. It slips from him.

Our big events slip from us like water.

There is one other time I heard a voice of presence coming after death, and again I keep forgetting about it, and again I had to write it down; and again there was no sound to it, but voice it was, nevertheless — a clear voice that imparted its meaning — and when I am given to return to those moments, it rings in memory, still.

In June of 1990, I wasn't at home, but living among strangers — other writers — in an unfamiliar rented house in the Colonial town of Duxbury, Massachusetts, along the Atlantic shore. Five or six women were there in mutual solitude, keeping to our own rooms in order to concentrate on our work. One day I got called downstairs to the telephone. It was my agent, her tone triumphant. My manuscript sprung from the trip to Germany with Robert three years before had just been "taken." If the next negotiation went as she expected, then the fourth novel I'd written was going to get published as my first book. The mix of elation and relief that swept through me buckled my knees. My life's long goal just met. Oh, I wanted to leap to the ceiling and dance a jig. I was at a new place now.

I phoned Rebecca back in Boston and we shouted together. The connection between us was so strong that it didn't matter right then that we were apart. "Can you tell anyone else yet?" she asked. "Are you kidding?" I replied, giddy. "Everyone."

I was so filled by energy that I couldn't stay still. Instead of sitting down and dialing, I got my bicycle, put on the helmet, and started out. The curves of the road turned me toward the pine woods and outward again toward the shore. The turns were taking me as swiftly as I took them. *Taken*, I thought, my novel has been *taken*. Yes had entered the conversation. Yes, where I'd heard no. The vistas kept flowing. Bent over the handlebars, I moved without thought, moved as one body lithe and near to flying, spending the speed of change as my charge.

When finally I braked and dismounted, I stood watching the waves spin against outcroppings of rocks. I took a deep breath and my lips were slick with the sting of salt. My eyes filled. As if from a distance, I heard myself weeping. I tugged off the safety helmet and the isolation it conferred. I could not stop crying. The sea breeze riffled my damp hair. A gentle hand. I wanted to be able to tell my grandmother, who had died the December before, about the great thing — the thing I had always wanted — it had just happened. I wanted to say, Nonny, my life is growing wider.

Why do we cry, a friend once asked, when we're happy or when we are given something beautiful? Why don't we just laugh?

The next morning, early, I tiptoed past the others' closed doors. The beach was right there, new as the day. It was peaceful, yet active. Sea wrack filigreed the high-tide mark. Gulls, white-winged and determined, dove straight down for the water. The sand hiccupped with the tiny exhalations of burrowing life. I walked south along the cool grains, the barely risen sun and the low curling waves to my left. At some point, humming, I stopped to look back. And that's when my grandmother moves to my side, standing between me and the water. I understand her presence as I understand my own. I recognize her in that instant where the air does not shift, but everything else about perception does. I turn my head and as I do, as my eyes sweep across to the water (but I somehow understand that the way to the waves is blocked — and she, blocking them, nods), some-body brushes my right arm. A hand slips against my right palm. I twist about in confusion. Papa? As real as is the light in the air — and as invisible — he grins in greeting. I flush, ashamed. For I think of my grandmother all the time, but I have not thought about my grandfather, not really, for years. That he is here, despite my forgetfulness — ! On either side of me there is amusement, tenderness, and a sort of wise pity at my shame and awkwardness. I look from one to the other, my hands held in theirs. The message I receive in uninterrupted silent stereo is: *We are together now. We are going to take a little walk again on a Sunday morning.*

I could have shoved them away. I could have decided that

what I heard and saw without physically hearing or seeing was a projection of my own longing. But I think Papa's immanence disallowed me the ease of that escape route. The intellect could not drown the experience.

I accepted their presence. I shook away how I must have appeared to anybody waking in one of the shore houses and turning in bed to lift the shade from a window. In silence, I allowed myself to step forward. Weeping, I walked slowly, arms held slightly out from my sides, hands cupped, facing straight ahead. After a while, as quietly as the tide, they receded.

In the afternoon I was at the desk in my little room when one of the other writers shouted up the staircase that the phone was for me. "It's your brother," she yelled. "He's calling from the city. I guess he means New York." The house had only one telephone, the old black wall unit mounted at the very back of the kitchen. Rapidly I descended three flights of tilting steps. The receiver, left hanging from its loopy dark cord to keep the connection open, was making slow orbits inches above the linoleum, mouthpiece clunking against the wall on each pass.

"Robert? Hey, hi! Sorry about the wait."

"Congratulations on the book," he sang out.

The night before I'd left a message on his home machine, but of course he hadn't been there to pick up the call. In the long months after Ron's death, he tried to get out and keep busy and social. He sounded happy and solid.

"Tell me everything," he said expansively, generously.

Stretching the cord over to the table, I grabbed one of the chairs. Then I started blabbing on and on in excruciating detail about my miraculous deal. About fifteen minutes into the conversation, the morning on the beach popped into my head. It was as if it were a dream, one already slipping under the sharp surface of life. "Wait," I said, stopping my own flow.

Since the experience had felt utterly momentous only a few hours before, I rushed into an account. I wanted to tell Rob about what happened, but at the same time I was ready for and would understand his laughter. In fact, I laughed as I related my confusion at finding myself standing on a beach between our grandparents, and again as I confided the sweetness I'd heard in the silence of the message: *We are together now. We are going to take a little walk again on a Sunday morning.*

There was a pregnant silence when I finished.

"What," I said. "What?"

Rob said almost curtly: "They are together now."

"What?" I stood up from the wobbly chair. I walked back to the body of the phone, the cord recoiling by twirls. I turned to the window over the counter. "What are you saying?"

It was true. Papa's grave had been moved a few days before. Our parents had had his casket dug up from the old cemetery and reburied in the new one — easier to visit — where Nonny's body lay. Rob had spoken with Mom and Dad yesterday and they'd told him. He said they'd been thinking about it for some time, and then an opportunity came up, but only if they moved quickly and purchased more plots in the same row. They bought five, for the family.

"Why didn't they tell me? No one told me."

"Oh," my brother said lightly, "someone did."

"You really think so?" I said, staring out the window into a view still strange to me.

Voyagers

Surely whoever speaks to me in the right voice,
him or her I shall follow,
As the water follows the moon, silently, with fluid steps,
anywhere around the globe.
— WALT WHITMAN

I had to work my way round to speaking of death. Maybe everyone does. I know that the closer I got to paying full attention to March 11, 1995, the day my brother died, the more I heard his voice returning. Page by page, the void I'd been staring at for so long began to fill with words — stories I spun (but he had shared the events), memories I held on to (but had constructed with him). Certain sayings were his, alone, and when I veered and jigged off track, I almost could hear his light snarl of "Oh, Sarah Bernhardt, enough!" or I would catch the bright tumble of his laughter in the air and turn my head toward it to find, glinting, an entire direction I had not considered.

The closer I got to recalling the day Robert died, the more the weight of his death dissolved. I hadn't thought it would work out like that, because caught for too long in the tumult of how much I missed him, my energy was lost to distraction and fear. I did not know how to tell his story to you. Moreover, I did not know how to tell it to myself. I felt only the pressure of not speaking the words that piled up inside me. No silence weighs more heavily than the one made of loss, and no silence is darker.

I took as my guide something that Robert once said to me

when he was ill and trying to find a way back into life. Just this: We have to start from where we are.

And so, the grief that followed my brother's death and which silenced my voice for four years lies in the chapters near the start of the book. If you were to orbit back around, you would find my mourning there, years of grief set down out of sequence, set on the page long before I could speak clearly of the death that they of course trailed in life. You've been holding those words in your hands the entire time, even as you moved past them. You hold them still, reaching this page, which seems an end, but likely is not.

Journeys make circles. You don't have to be lost to know that.

Sometimes I think about the two small craft we long ago launched in the air. I think of them moving in silence, holding their wealth on a gold disk pledged to their sides. And I wonder how they are faring.

I have faith. I am calling hello.

Sources

The following are a few of the works whose contributions were important to the evolution of this book. I would especially like to credit:

Ancient Secrets: Using the Stories of the Bible to Improve Our Everyday Lives, Rabbi Levi Meier, Villard Books, 1996.

Breathing: The Source of Life: The Diaphragm in Motion (videotape), Carl Stough Institute, 1996.

"Journey to the Center of My Mind," Stephen S. Hall, *New York Times Magazine,* June 6, 1999.

Kaddish, Leon Wieseltier, Knopf, 1998.

Memory: Remembering and Forgetting in Everyday Life, Barry Gordon, M.D., Mastermedia Books, 1995.

A Natural History of the Senses, Diane Ackerman, Random House, 1990.

The 1999 Redstone Diary of the Millennium, Julian Rothenstein, Mel Gooding, editors, Redstone/Chronicle Books, 1998.

The Queen's Throat: Opera, Homosexuality, and the Mystery of Desire, Wayne Koestenbaum, Poseidon Press, 1993.

Stalking Elijah: Adventures with Today's Jewish Mystical Masters, Rodger Kamenetz, HarperSanFrancisco, 1997.

The Story of the Human Voice, Bill Severn, David McKay Co., 1961.

Voyage to Jupiter, David Morrison, Jane Samz; NASA Scientific and Technical Information Branch, National Aeronautics and Space Administration, 1980.

White Gloves: How We Create Ourselves Through Memory,
John Kotre, Free Press, 1995.
The Wisdom of Depression, Jonathan Zuess, Harmony Books,
1998.

Acknowledgments

During the course of writing this book, I was fortunate in my conversations with a number of people. In particular, I am grateful for the encouragement and literary insights of Eileen Pollack, Margot Livesey, Suzanne Berne, Olga Broumas, Anita Diamant, Ellen Grabiner, Amy Hoffman, Michelle Green, Judith Bolton-Fasman, Lee Edelman, Thane Rosenbaum, and my agent, Ellen Levine. To my editor, Deborah Chasman, who asked for this book and expertly guided it, thank you beyond measure.

And to all those who spoke to me with such generosity about their interactions with Robert, you know, don't you? I thank you.